The New York Times

BEST OF THURSDAY CROSSWORDS

The New York Times

BEST OF THURSDAY CROSSWORDS
75 of Your Favorite Tricky Thursday Puzzles from *The New York Times*

Edited by Will Shortz

ST. MARTIN'S GRIFFIN ✠ NEW YORK

The New York Times

SMART PUZZLES

Presented with Style

ACROSS

1 Eye
5 Clothing retailer on the New York Stock Exchange since 2006
10 Casa ___, Toronto castle
14 Andy Roddick, at times
15 "A Dog of Flanders" novelist, 1872
16 Rapper with the gold-record album "O.G. Original Gangster"
17 Tiny sideshow attraction
19 Juggling nine balls, e.g.
20 "___ me, that's who!"
21 Short race, for short
22 Cyberball maker
23 Old weather forecaster
27 ___ Bridge, first to span the Mississippi at St. Louis
28 Shorten, as a sail
29 Israel's Olmert
32 City nicknamed Gateway to the West
36 When a big game is caught
40 Remove, as a mustache
41 Title film role for Robin Williams
42 Make
43 Place for pins
46 Roosevelt group
52 Guiding beliefs
53 "___ bien"
54 Sue Grafton's "___ for Outlaw"
56 Win
57 Where things are freely bought and sold . . . and what the starts of 17-, 23-, 36- and 46-Across do?

60 Celtic language
61 ___ Montoya, DC Comics heroine known as the Question
62 First name in horror
63 Fly catcher
64 ___ squash
65 Movie hero with a fedora, familiarly

DOWN

1 Daily trippers?
2 Sign of treble?
3 Radio host Gibbons
4 History text unit
5 Wedded
6 Shamans
7 Gin joint in "Casablanca"
8 End of a professor's address
9 Is in the past

10 Do anything to help
11 Place to use an echograph
12 Half of a popular comedy team
13 Ancient Greek
18 What a person who's out may be in
22 "I'd like to see ___"
24 Like land in urban renewal
25 Seed case
26 Projector part
29 Switchback shape
30 "Say what?"
31 ___ tree
32 Former grapplers' org.
33 Palm Pilot, e.g., briefly
34 Iowa harvest unit
35 Con
37 Stationer's stock

38 Queens, e.g., informally
39 ___ consequence
43 "Wouldn't It Be Loverly" lyricist
44 Missing links?
45 Columbia org.
46 Arty topper
47 Unborn, after "in"
48 Disputed holy city
49 Pool temp, maybe
50 Bit of arcade currency
51 Return
55 A judge might issue one
57 ___ pro nobis
58 Muscle builder's muscle, for short
59 Big stat for Manny Ramirez

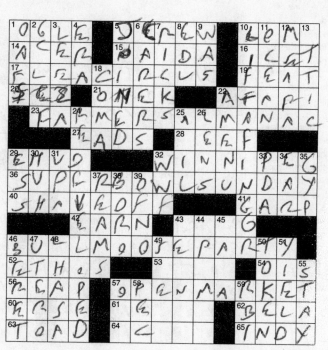

by James Sajdak

2

ACROSS

1 Give a majority of the vote
6 "Semper Fidelis" composer
11 Feature of a peacock's tail
14 Instrument often played while sitting on the floor
15 "The uncertain glory of an ___ day": Shakespeare
16 ___ Percé tribe
17 Precious moments
19 Filch
20 Drunkard
21 Arizona county or river
22 Seemingly endless
25 Phrase from which the exclamation "Zounds!" comes
29 Notes in C minor chords
31 Goes quietly
32 Red in the face, maybe
33 Like ___ in the head
35 Motto derived from Virgil
41 Lift
42 French menu phrase
43 Some neighborhoods
47 Neighbor of Francia
48 Dominatrix's wear
51 Form of the Latin "esse"
52 ___ facto
53 Peninsular nation
55 Actor Billy ___ Williams
56 Speaker of the quip revealed by the ends of the answers to 17-, 25-, 35- and 48-Across
62 Inner ___
63 Murphy of "The Red Badge of Courage"

64 End of a railing
65 Some yearbook signers: Abbr.
66 Arthur Murray instruction
67 China's Zhou

DOWN

1 Atty.'s title
2 Sch. in Brooklyn
3 Cockpit guess, for short
4 Fullerton campus
5 ZZ Top, e.g.
6 Unsupported statement
7 Chose
8 Canton bordering Valais
9 Computer family member
10 Bar choice

11 San Fernando Valley community
12 Start of many an English inn's name
13 Thruway convenience
18 Yanks
21 Kind of instinct
22 Maugham's "The Painted ___"
23 ___-American
24 Dweller along the Danube
26 Bar choice
27 Chicanery
28 Met expectations?
30 Geek Squad member
33 Flavoring for pfeffernüsse
34 Command centers: Abbr.
36 "How exciting!"
37 George Reeves and Christopher Reeve

38 Admitting just a little light, maybe
39 ___ moth
40 Its max. score is 180
43 They're opposite hits
44 Materialize
45 Choral platforms
46 Studio of "Notorious" and "Suspicion"
47 Book before Job: Abbr.
49 Rig out
50 They're found above tongues
54 Dynamite
56 Rightmost pedal
57 Sticking point
58 W. H. Auden wrote one to his pupils
59 It has a sticking point
60 New Deal inits.
61 Year Claudius I became emperor

by Alex Boisvert

ACROSS

1 France's ___ von Bismarck
5 Jumped
11 Rogue
14 Chemical element with the symbol Fe
15 Sub
16 Discounted item: Abbr.
17 Gets it wrong
18 Terrible one?
19 Former pharmaceutical giant
20 Flow slowly
21 Flat things?
22 Out of: Ger.
23 Sum derives from it
24 Father of Jacob
25 Monopoly quartet: Abbr.
26 Spot
31 Preemie setting: Abbr.
32 Suffix with palm
33 Collection of teams
36 Crane, e.g.
39 Possible name for the first decade of the century
40 Hold back
41 Hardly soothes
42 Former Romanian leader Ion ___
43 One step from the majors
44 Nickname on the Houston Rockets starting in 2004
45 Kind of dog
51 Solution strength: Abbr.
52 Road access regulators
53 Sooner
54 Always bouncing back
55 Places for La-Z-Boys

56 Number of clues in this puzzle that contain factual inaccuracies
57 Dwarf planet larger than Pluto

DOWN

1 "I'll be with you shortly . . ."
2 Mother of Calcutta
3 One way to lay things
4 Uncommissioned
5 Silverstein who wrote and illustrated "The Giving Tree"
6 Corn dish
7 San ___, Calif.
8 Golf great Andre
9 Standard office-closing time
10 Arises

11 One who exhibits pack mentality?
12 Who quipped "God tells me how the music should sound, but you stand in the way"
13 Job seeker's fashion advice
27 Bolt
28 It's more than 90°
29 "Nope, still not right"
30 Writing that's hard to read
33 Mill input
34 Part of E.E.C.: Abbr.
35 Turkish pooh-bah
36 Verdi's "___ tu"
37 Th.D. subj.
38 Prefix with center
45 Narrow passage: Abbr.

46 Job ad abbr.
47 Tennis champ Ernie
48 Time to lie in le soleil?
49 Currency of China
50 Summer hrs. in N.Y.C.

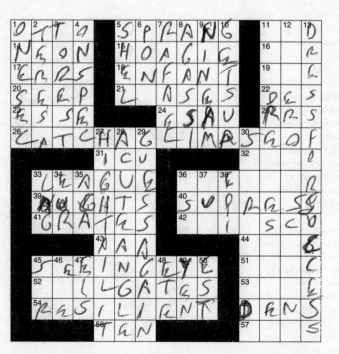

by Joe Krozel

ACROSS

1 Omani's money
5 It circles Hades nine times
9 Pro Football Hall of Fame coach who once played for the New York Yankees
14 Spanish pronoun
15 Runoff site
16 Airport rental option
17 Rube's opposite
19 Circle lines
20 Lets out
21 New York's ___ Building, tallest in the world in 1930
22 Agonizes (over)
23 Submarine base?
25 Want ad letters
26 Graduated
28 Figs. in sports reports
31 See 7-Down
33 "Paradise Lost," e.g.
34 "Upidstay" language
37 Girl's name that's a butterfly genus
38 First name in erotic writing
39 Tow truck tool
42 Two- or three-year-old, maybe
43 Product introduced by 7-Down in 1971
45 Photography abbr.
46 "___ Mistress," 1982 horror flick
47 One for the road
50 1974 hit by Mocedades
52 Dog from Japan
54 Check attachments
56 What may be paid when someone dies

59 Make ___ with the devil
60 Extra shuteye
61 Bank manager?
62 Stud fee?
63 River to the English Channel
64 Push (oneself)
65 Wee, informally
66 Liz Taylor's husband before Fisher

DOWN

1 Disqualify in court
2 Enjoys a lot
3 Potsdam Conference attendee
4 Knocks to the ground
5 Short moments
6 Receipts
7 Legendary name in 31-Across
8 See 37-Down

9 Sarcastic laugh
10 Bank feature
11 Orchid variety
12 Gallic girlfriend
13 It may be "bon"
18 Cyclades isle
21 Reunion group
24 Phone greeting in Central America
26 Former fleet member
27 Cub's home, for short
29 One of the Jacksons
30 Word with brain or price
31 Dart
32 Some batteries
33 Canal near Rome
34 Gait
35 Privy to
36 "Ben-Hur" extra
37 With 8-Down, one who grew up on MTV, maybe

40 Discontinued Saturn
41 Some QB protectors
43 Whom Taylor defeated for president in 1848
44 Giant among Giants
46 Wedding band, maybe
47 "De Oratore" writer
48 Take care of
49 Scraped
51 Kitchen gizmo
52 Suitable
53 Lock opening
54 Prone to freckles
55 Ne plus ultra
57 Grub
58 Chop ___
60 Actress ___ Ling of "Sky Captain and the World of Tomorrow"

by David J. Kahn

5

ACROSS

1. "___ Si Bon" (1950s Eartha Kitt hit)
5. Post-diet, ideally
9. Surfaces
14. Dinosaur National Monument locale
15. ___ bar
16. "Scenes of Clerical Life" author, 1858
17. 1958 World Cup hero
18. 50-50
19. See 24-Across
20. What this answer could use?
23. Record producer Brian
24. With 19-Across, language from which "steak" and "eggs" come
25. On intimate social terms with
28. Alaska vacation destination
30. Spray on a pan
32. Federally funded program since '65
33. Coiner
35. Coin toss call
37. Like this answer's error
40. Upset
41. Prize
42. Un cuarto of 62-Across
43. Compete in a biathlon, in part
44. "Sweet ___"
48. Sound choice?
51. "Years ___ . . ."
52. ___ Jemison, first black woman in space
53. This answer contains one
57. Top celebs
59. Jordanian queen
60. Queen of the heavens
61. Hanukkah staple
62. Cuatro times 42-Across
63. Help with a prank
64. "___ Eyes" (1969 hit)
65. Irwin who wrote "Rich Man, Poor Man"
66. Took in

DOWN

1. Like beggars' hands
2. Timeless, to Shakespeare
3. Watering hole
4. One of the "Cosby Show" kids
5. First-rate
6. Long-___
7. Company founded by Ingvar Kamprad
8. Take exception to
9. Pasta choice
10. Isolated
11. Atlantic Coast Conference team
12. Mother of the stars and the winds
13. ___-Julie, Que.
21. Page numbers
22. Tour's end?
26. Dudley Do-Right's girlfriend
27. Ozone, for one
29. Concert hall equipment
30. It "hits the spot" per an old jingle
31. "Was it ___ I saw?" (classic palindrome)
34. Migration, maybe
35. Steering system part
36. Pinnacle
37. Instruction at a horse show
38. Home of the 1,612-foot Ribbon Falls
39. Property divider
40. Music sources
43. Saturate
45. Tiny blob
46. Defective
47. Calm
49. Takes a chance on
50. First name in beauty products
51. "Hawaii ___" (island song)
54. "The Dukes of Hazzard" spinoff
55. Scotland's ___ Awe
56. Pow!
57. PC key
58. ___-di-dah

by Keith Talon

6

ACROSS

1 Gave an order to
5 Fork
10 Woods call
14 Platinum Card offerer, for short
15 Shopping center
16 Shuffle or 67-Across, e.g.
17 Eliminate, with "out"
18 Symbol of thinness
19 Alternatives to creams
20 Arctic explorer post-fight?
23 Hatch or Byrd: Abbr.
24 Formerly, in high society
25 Possible cover for a siesta
27 Mood
29 Some offensive linemen: Abbr.
32 Off
33 "___ Love," 1975 Jackson 5 hit
35 "THAT guy!"
37 Past
38 Bows and arrows for Midas?
43 Was on the ticket
44 Major Indonesian export
45 Big inits. in Hollywood
46 1985 John Malkovich drama
49 Beseech
51 Convinced
54 Choice poultry
56 Use (up), as savings
58 Common suffix on chemical elements
60 Storage area for ribbed fabric?
64 Ladies' man
65 Inspector of crime fiction
66 Yearn (for)
67 See 16-Across
68 Model
69 Horse-drawn carriage
70 Switch possibilities
71 Level . . . or a three-word hint to 20-, 38- and 60-Across
72 Proctor's call

DOWN

1 Unpleasant remarks
2 Item worn around the neck, maybe
3 Presidential middle name
4 Prez, e.g.
5 Binge at the mall
6 Ladies' man
7 What many do on a day off
8 Polo alternative
9 Temporary covers
10 Singer of Rossini's "Largo al factotum"
11 Zero personality?
12 Pudgy
13 Money managers?: Abbr.
21 Massage
22 Night of poetry
26 Tight ___
28 Not even a little
30 Shakespearean title
31 English title
34 Big Apple cultural attraction, with "the"
36 Hosts
38 Enormous
39 Candy box size
40 Pen point
41 "___ mañana"
42 The "I" of Claudius I
43 Boombox button
47 Like some skiing
48 Not the party type?: Abbr.
50 Yellowstone Park attraction
52 Chinese fruit tree
53 Duke's home
55 Water pits
57 Copycatting
59 "The hell you say!"
61 Source
62 Roughly
63 Thomas with a pointed pen
64 Little, to Robert Burns

by Ari Halpern

ACROSS

1 Salt or smoke
5 Starr of the Old West
10 Boom
14 Type type: Abbr.
15 Bay window
16 ___ colada
17 Like a bell
18 Pale purple
19 Pancake Day is the day before this begins
20 Make rustle, as foil
22 Writes odes to, e.g.
24 U.N. secretary general from Ghana
25 Not straight up
26 Bits
29 Winter melon
33 Colorful lawn or garden fixture
37 Soundtrack annoyance
38 Slithering danger
39 Hebrews, for example
43 A pitcher should keep it low
44 Something you might want to get to the heart of?
46 Annoy
50 Sale day feeling
51 They cross here
53 ___ salts
57 One of TV's Gilmore Girls
60 Unfolds
62 Pen pal in Paris, perhaps
63 Agreement
65 Exercised a legal option
66 Police protection
67 Doha's domain
68 "___ This Last" (series of John Ruskin essays)
69 ___ place
70 Stood out, in a good way
71 Say no

DOWN

1 Around
2 Often-illegal maneuver
3 Entered quickly
4 Percussion instrument in an orchestra
5 Cotton pod
6 Pennsylvania's northwesternmost county
7 One of TV's Rugrats
8 Bounded
9 Coterie
10 Forks
11 "The Worst ___ in London" ("Sweeney Todd" song)
12 Monarch immediately after William and Mary
13 Headliner
21 Small hill
23 Mobile home?: Abbr.
25 "___ see it . . ."
27 Railroad crossbeam
28 Tourist city between Jaipur and Lucknow
30 Middle range
31 Hesitate
32 Author James
33 Bird with speckled eggs
34 Fabled racer
35 "Take ___ face value"
36 "___ life!"
40 Fraternity jewelry
41 More likely to cause slipping
42 Quits misbehaving . . . or a literal hint to 4-, 9-, 13-, 49- and 57-Down
45 Abbr. in real estate ads
47 Chirps
48 Ha-ha, nowadays
49 Unhip person
52 Alice's pet cat in "Alice in Wonderland"
54 Hot spot
55 "The Country Girl" playwright, 1950
56 Many PCs once ran on it
57 Racetrack
58 Impending clouds, e.g.
59 Small hill
60 Avant-garde filmmaker Brakhage
61 Funeral sight
64 "What am ___ do?"

by Elizabeth A. Long

ACROSS

1 Warm-blooded shark
5 Blood's partner
10 Klingon on "Star Trek: T.N.G."
14 With 46-Down, writer of "The Autobiography of Malcolm X"
15 Originator of the equation $e^{i\pi} + 1 = 0$
16 Airline that doesn't fly on Saturday
17 Hollow-point projectiles
19 Title cocker spaniel in a Disney film
20 Bazaar
21 Pixie-esque
22 Mutually beneficial interaction
25 Roughly triangular racket
28 Chemistry Nobelist Hahn, who co-discovered nuclear fission
29 "___ Majesty" (last track on "Abbey Road")
30 Reconciled
35 Jacqueline Susann novel, and the problem with some of the answers in this puzzle
39 Follows temporally
40 Order at a French restaurant
41 Berlin article
42 Delight
45 Puerto Rican-born P.G.A. star
50 Lacks, briefly
51 Impoverished
55 "___ Want for Christmas"
56 Child's fair-weather wish
58 Usher's offer
59 Agreeing (with)
60 "Your Majesty"
61 "Really!"
62 Annual awards presented in Los Angeles
63 Legis. meeting

DOWN

1 Synthetic
2 Fund-raising target, briefly
3 Dole's 1996 running mate
4 River bends
5 Like a leopard
6 Beauts
7 Incense resin
8 Volleyball action before a spike
9 9 a.m. and 5 p.m.
10 Rich
11 Norwegian king who converted the Vikings to Christianity
12 Portion of an advertising budget
13 One of the Mudville players on base when the mighty Casey struck out
18 "Trinity" author
21 Taken in
23 Tugboat warnings
24 ___ Reader
25 Dice, say
26 Slots spot
27 "The Lord of the Rings" army
30 Lay to rest
31 Preschoolers?
32 "I'm Gonna Wash That Man Right ___ My Hair"
33 Oral grimaces
34 What you used to be
36 Forever
37 "You ___!" (cry while hitting oneself on the head)
38 Levee material
42 Mass dismissals
43 Duke Atreides in "Dune"
44 New York bridge toll option
45 Wide divide
46 See 14-Across
47 Its symbol is a crescent moon
48 Go for broke, e.g.
49 ___ Weasley of Harry Potter books
52 Toddler's cry of pain
53 They're found in banks
54 Bar stock
56 Charlotte of "The Facts of Life"
57 Cash cache

by Matt Ginsberg

ACROSS

1 Temple activity
8 Tex-Mex treats
15 Wedding gown material
16 Distinguished
17 Dean Martin, for one
18 Bach work
19 1979 Bee Gees chart-topper
21 Civvies
23 ___ change
24 QB's stat.
25 Great Plains tribe
26 County of St. Andrews, Scotland
28 Part of a seal
30 Professor Lupin in Harry Potter books, e.g.
33 Creator of the Bennet family
34 Band with the 1970 hit "Get Ready"
36 One of the four evangelists, briefly
39 Many Latin compositions
43 Come up
44 Shot (off)
45 Yes, in Yokohama
46 Let go
47 Author of a once-popular book of quotations
48 Devil
50 1979 AC/DC seven-time platinum album
55 Blow up
56 Emit
59 Smaller than small
60 Where the buoys are?
61 Puts under
62 Takes over

DOWN

1 Fighters' org.
2 1967 N.H.L. rookie of the year
3 Support, at a game
4 Tear out
5 Radio ___ (onetime propaganda source)
6 Footnote word
7 Locale for Che Guevara in "The Motorcycle Diaries"
8 Computer whiz
9 Menotti title character
10 Harbor danger
11 Architectural pier
12 Michael ___, Bush secretary of health and human services
13 Accord
14 Suffragist Elizabeth Cady ___
20 One that's "perky" in the morning
21 Shorten, in a way
22 Multipurpose truck
26 Chess tactic that involves attacking two pieces at once
27 Spot in la mer
28 Half-and-half, maybe
29 Department of Labor agcy.
31 Post-Civil War Reconstruction and others
32 Pottery
33 Unimaginative
35 Koko who communicates through American Sign Language, e.g.
36 Lingerie drawer items
37 Drill instructor's charge
38 Got around at a get-together
40 Military wing
41 Eggs Benedict ingredient
42 Hardly a chug
44 Football Hall-of-Famer Gale
47 Patrick ___, 1996 Tony recipient for "Marat/Sade"
48 Q45 or Grand Marquis
49 "Walkin' After Midnight" hitmaker, 1957
51 Mandlikova of tennis fame
52 Judicial directive
53 Killer whale
54 Violin virtuoso Hilary
57 Gadget for 58-Down
58 Golfer dubbed "the Big Easy"

by Allan E. Parrish

10

ACROSS
1 Quatrain form
5 Latin lover's word?
9 BlackBerry output: Abbr.
13 Co-star of the film whose title is hidden sequentially in 20-, 34-, 41- and 52-Across
15 Inflict upon
16 Squabbling
17 "Not so loud!"
19 Costa ___, Calif.
20 About to collapse, say
22 DHL delivery: Abbr.
23 Subject for Freud
24 Amu ___, Asian river
27 Singles players
30 When brunch may be scheduled
33 Poetic preposition
34 Plea from the plate
37 Some yeses
39 Like some columns
40 Take off
41 Canine coat
44 Apt name for a fiftyish Roman woman?
45 Show host
46 It makes pets pests
47 Usher's domain
49 Eliot Ness, notably, for short
51 Bull Halsey in W.W. II, e.g.: Abbr.
52 Some W.W. I code talkers
59 Leaf feature
60 Aesthetically pleasing ratio of antiquity
62 German-built auto
63 Verdi's "Di Provenza il mar," e.g.
64 Another co-star of the film hidden in this puzzle
65 Beatles song that begins "Is there anybody going to listen to my story"
66 Hard wood
67 Point out

DOWN
1 Not the main rte.
2 "To ___ not to . . ."
3 Japanese aborigine
4 Spook's employer, with "the"
5 Wing: Abbr.
6 Eponymous instrument maker Robert
7 Retired Audi supermini
8 British weight
9 Giant tusk holders
10 Items unlikely to be stored on the top shelf
11 Essence
12 Command to Fido
14 Suggest
18 Anniversary gift for the year after pottery
21 Was at the Colosseum?
24 Al ___
25 Get ___ for the night
26 Object of a hunt in a 1984 best seller
27 Queen's subject?
28 ___ Brothers (pop trio)
29 Dips
31 What a server may serve
32 Brass
35 Get shaking
36 Hotel freebie
38 Subject of modern research
42 Coppers
43 Bill of ___ (shipping document)
48 1965 Yardbirds hit
50 Pester
51 It's made in a squeeze
52 Backup cause
53 Literally, "peaceful" person
54 Eroded
55 Hip bones
56 Locale of Sitting Bull Coll.
57 Mountain where Moses died, in the Bible
58 Curer
61 Alumna identifier

by Peter A. Collins and Joe Krozel

Note: When this puzzle is done, unscramble the five circled letters to find out how the circles could have been left with the puzzle's solution still being correct.

ACROSS

1 Mythical hammer wielder
5 Nickname for a namesake of Mary's husband
9 Burn, in a way
14 ___ wave
15 First name in folk
16 "Institutiones Calculi Integralis" writer
17 Castle stronghold
18 Like some interest
20 Unauthorized preview, say
22 Ocasek of the Cars
23 Apology starter
24 Resettle
28 Serious
30 Strip joint, euphemistically
31 My ___
32 Joan Miró's "L'___"
33 Prefix for many cold-weather product names
34 Glacial ridges
38 Like 1-Across
41 Lee of Hollywood
43 Position
44 Part of a veterinarian's job
46 Aegean island near Naxos
48 The Tigers of the Ohio Valley Conf.
49 General for whom a style of chicken is named
50 Crab
53 Roly-poly
56 Defiling
57 German pronoun
58 Lawyers' org.
60 Faithful, to a Scot
61 Went on
65 Goddess in the hand of the statue of Athena in the Parthenon
68 Poe-ish
69 Call to Rover
70 Taking care of things
71 Some histrionics
72 Career division, in sports
73 Capt.'s inferiors

DOWN

1 Finger wagger's sound
2 Speed
3 Comic's stock
4 Adjusts, as a currency rate
5 Crooks' lackeys
6 Sch. in Tulsa, Okla.
7 State tree of Massachusetts
8 Not their
9 Port locale
10 Director's cry
11 Out on ___
12 It holds water
13 Gloomy, literarily
19 Thread type
21 Fly ball's path
24 Fix
25 Little brother's cry, perhaps
26 Deli sandwich choice
27 Vernacular that came into prominence in 1996
29 One of a candy box duo
35 Making necessary
36 Balsam, e.g.
37 Burned
39 In ___ (positioned naturally)
40 Tangles
42 Sticky stuff
45 "___ with you" (parting words)
47 Smoke a little
51 "American ___"
52 Grasslands
53 More red, maybe
54 Papery sheath on a plant stem
55 Protective protrusion
59 Wan
62 "Shoo!"
63 Match
64 Reconstruction, e.g.
66 Do-it-yourselfer's aid
67 Uranians, e.g., in brief

by Damon J. Gulczynski

12

ACROSS

1 Capital on Lake Victoria
8 Morrow and Murrow, e.g.
15 Part of a floor décor
16 War movie sound effect
17 Innards
18 Hostility
19 Musical group that stays together?
21 Bulldogger's event
22 Herd : buffalo :: Knot : ___
26 Part of Eastern Europe, once: Abbr.
29 Cryptanalysis org.
32 Ancient theaters
33 Mountain West Conference player
34 Faith healing service?
38 Iowa county named for an Indian tribe
39 Death on the Nile cause?
40 Thurman of the "Kill Bill" films
41 Frolicsome
42 Stadium's dome?
45 Home of Samuel Beckett: Abbr.
46 Designer Saab
47 Beach shade
48 Red Cross supply
49 City near Dayton
51 Infatuation
55 Donation to the Salvation Army?
61 1960s sitcom title role
64 Three-dimensional scene
65 Played the role of
66 Ready to blow
67 Most brazen
68 Eternal . . . and a hint to 19-, 34-, 42- and 55-Across

DOWN

1 Intoxicating Polynesian drink
2 Parched
3 Jersey material
4 Bankers Life Fieldhouse team
5 "Am not!" rejoinder
6 Shocking
7 Tequila source
8 Chi-town daily, with "the"
9 Cow: Sp.
10 Tour of duty
11 It's hot in an Indian restaurant
12 Put away
13 Univ. dorm supervisors
14 G.P.S. data: Abbr.
20 Stretches of history
23 How "Moon River" is played
24 Take off
25 Give permission
26 Northernmost county in New Jersey
27 Chase scenes, in action films
28 Bring back, as silver dollars
30 String before W
31 "Whatever shall I do?!"
34 Ring surface
35 Entry-level position: Abbr.
36 Pet lovers' org.
37 Plug place
43 Held sway
44 One way to store data
48 Beethoven's ___ Symphony
50 Former "Biography" channel
52 "___ cock-horse to Banbury Cross"
53 Not abstaining
54 Germ
56 Narrow inlets
57 Oscar superlative
58 Brush material?
59 ___ Building, first skyscraper in Boston
60 Schoolboys
61 Boxer's setup
62 Prefix with -cide
63 U.S./U.K. divider

by Gary J. Whitehead

ACROSS

1 Poor dating prospects
5 Central Africa's Lake ___
9 Place for a motto
14 M.P.'s quarry
15 Bloody, so to speak
16 Early British automaker Henry
17 Hot strip?
18 Washington has some big ones
19 Mountaineering equipment
20 Historical 1976 miniseries
23 $C_7H_5N_3O_6$
24 Toy at the beach
25 Close, old-style
27 Record holder
30 Refrigerator part
32 Big name in Gotham City
33 "Mens sana in corpore ___"
34 California's ___ Music Festival, since 1947
36 Goon
37 Juliet, e.g., in Gounod's "Romeo and Juliet"
40 Chapel Hill sch.
41 Only player to be part of three World Cup-winning teams
43 Poland's second-largest city
44 Tear
46 Obeys
48 Didn't raise
49 ___ light: Var.
50 Lay person?
51 Reverence
53 Punny hint to answering 20-Across, 11-Down and 29-Down
58 Sends
60 Object of ridicule
61 After-lunch bite
62 Black tea
63 Stick on a dish
64 Scraggy
65 It may be rounded up in a roundup
66 European capital
67 "Do the Right Thing" pizzeria

DOWN

1 Part of a pound
2 Out
3 Siesta
4 Abate
5 Hatch
6 Global legal venue, with "The"
7 Yankee nickname starting in 2004
8 1940s–'50s film/TV star with two stars on the Hollywood Walk of Fame
9 Cause for using a hot line
10 Sinbad's avian attacker
11 Classic 1947 detective novel
12 Process, in a way, as documents
13 Transcript
21 Biographies
22 ___ Station
26 Delivery notation: Abbr.
27 Give and take
28 It's sometimes grabbed
29 Bygone political slogan
30 '06 Series winner
31 Eastern royal
33 Title TV character in Bikini Bottom
35 Put away
38 Liquid fat
39 Prefix with sclerosis
42 Night school class, for short
45 Soldiers' jobs
47 Come-on
48 Not punishing sufficiently
50 One of the "Brady Bunch" kids
51 Cold-blooded killers
52 Stimulate
54 Holiday season
55 Quarter
56 "Hud" Oscar winner
57 Ones with charges
59 Writer who wrote "I became insane, with long intervals of horrible sanity"

by Sheldon Benardo

ACROSS

1 Feature of an acacia tree
6 1986 showbiz autobiography
11 W.W. II hero, for short
14 Historical biography that won a 1935 Pulitzer
15 & 16 Boxing result, often
17 Certain feed
18 Slow
20 Delphic quality
22 Hawaii's annual ___ Bowl
23 & 24 Curious case in psychology
26 Free
28 Watch brand
32 Where Nixon went to law school
35 Much of central Eur., once
36 Life, liberty and the pursuit of happiness
37 Married
38 & 39 Instant
40 Nod, say
41 Sped (by)
43 G.R.E. takers, generally: Abbr.
44 Locale for four World Series
45 The last 10% of 110%
46 Three-wheeled Indian taxi
48 & 50 Grammatical infelicities
54 Quiet cough
57 From southern Spain
59 Patent holder's income
61 Total
62 & 63 Go Dutch
64 Comparatively considerate
65 Seed alternative

66 They're usually washed separately
67 Medical flow enhancer

DOWN

1 "The Sound of Music" name
2 Soixante minutes
3 "Wait till you're ___" (parent's reply)
4 Bing Crosby's "White Christmas," again and again
5 Hawk, maybe
6 Lay off
7 Pubescent, say
8 Makeshift dagger
9 American-born Japanese
10 The Sun Devils, for short
11 Diable battler
12 Sweetie

13 Irish singer with eight platinum U.S. albums
19 Trample, for example
21 Proceeded slowly
25 Former E.P.A. chief Christine ___ Whitman
27 It's produced by a Tesla coil
29 Singly
30 Affix
31 Where Melville's Billy Budd went
32 Not be alert
33 Operating system developed at Bell Labs
34 Stayed fresh
36 Impart gradually: Var.
38 Grammy-winning reggae artist ___ Paul
39 TV planet
42 ___ facie
43 Tanner's locale

44 Attire that often includes a hood
46 More minute
47 Flip-flops
49 Jazz's Earl Hines, familiarly
51 Wrestling promoter McMahon
52 Gone, in a way
53 Bar belt
54 Wiles
55 Twinkie alternative
56 Assessed visually
58 Poses posers
60 Plasma alternative, briefly

by Matt Ginsberg

When this puzzle is done, connect the circled letters in alphabetical order, and then back to the start, to reveal something seen on the 32-Down 4-Down.

ACROSS

1 Waxed
5 First name in erotica
10 They might be chocolate
14 ___ Flynn Boyle of "Twin Peaks"
15 Request at a laundry
16 Like some keys
17 Dye plant
18 Popular women's fragrance
19 Together, in music
20 Makes people offers they can't refuse?
22 Apportionment
23 Set of values
24 View from Marseille
25 Relatives, slangily
27 You might end up with a bum one
30 Actress Tyler
31 Child, for one
34 Adler who outwitted Sherlock Holmes
36 ___ impulse
38 ___ + grenadine + maraschino cherry = Roy Rogers cocktail
39 Illumination of manuscripts, and others
40 Headline-making illness of 2002–03
41 Dis
42 Mushroom maker, for short
43 Tony nominee for "Glengarry Glen Ross"
44 Interrogator's discovery
45 Cultural org.
46 Retain
48 Rand who created Dagny Taggart
49 Striped quartz
53 ___ pop, music genre since the 1980s
55 Nocturnal bloodsucker
60 Tony Musante TV series
61 Extracted chemical
62 Punishment unit
63 Frost
64 Options during computer woes
65 James of jazz
66 Competitor of Ben & Jerry's
67 "Thus . . ."
68 Spotted

DOWN

1 Ruiner of many a photo
2 Charged
3 Filmmaker Von Stroheim
4 Theme of this puzzle
5 Without ___ (riskily)
6 It may be wrinkled
7 Ancient Semitic fertility goddess
8 Bakery employee
9 Elvis Presley's "___ Not You"
10 Detective's need
11 Like some six-packs
12 See 32-Down
13 Vile smile
21 That, to Tomás
26 Home of "The Last Supper"
27 Place for picnicking and dog-walking
28 Hill dwellers
29 ___ alla Genovese (sauce)
30 City where 32- and 12-Down is found
31 Also sends to, as an e-mail
32 With 12-Down, locale of the 4-Down
33 "Ishtar" director
35 You might give a speech by this
37 Ultrasecret org.
47 "That mad game the world so loves to play," to Jonathan Swift
48 ___ ready
50 Peter out
51 It's often unaccounted for
52 Allen in American history
54 All ___
55 Lynn who sang "We'll Meet Again"
56 Port near the Red Sea
57 Yellow squirt?
58 Pie chart figs.
59 "Wishing won't make ___"

by Caleb Madison

16

ACROSS

1 Eric's "Will & Grace" co-star
6 Language from which "divan" is derived
11 Dunderhead
14 Thin as ___
15 Strand, somehow
16 Nickname for #6 on the Sixers
17 [See circles]
19 D.D.E.'s W.W. II command
20 Well-dressed, photogenic male
21 [See circles]
23 Delays set them back: Abbr.
25 "No horsing around!"
26 Negligent
29 A.B.A. member's title
30 Burger order
31 "How Do ___" (1997 LeAnn Rimes hit)
33 One pointing and clicking
35 Oenophile's interest
39 80, for Hg
40 Northern Europeans
41 Start time for many a military mission
42 Colonel's div.
43 Check box option on a Spanish survey?
44 "Dream Lover" singer, 1959
45 CNBC news topics, for short
47 Business with a register
49 Paris's Basilique ___-Clotilde
50 Language that treats "dz" as a single consonant
53 Use a cell phone outside one's calling area

55 [See circles]
58 Recess
62 Dick
63 [See circles]
65 Egypt's ___ Simbel historical site
66 Defensive retort
67 Scottish child
68 Seedy sort?
69 Majority of a crowd at a Jonas Brothers concert
70 "I'm outta here!"

DOWN

1 Family pet in "Hi and Lois"
2 Former "ER" co-star La Salle
3 Having one's heart set (on)
4 Change colors?
5 Oliver Twist, for one

6 Hi-___
7 Result of overstrain
8 Concrete
9 Court huddles
10 Taken-aback response
11 Start of many dedications
12 ___-Detoo
13 Finger of the ocean
18 Forms a union
22 Program
24 Occupies an abandoned building
26 Either of two guests on "To Tell the Truth"
27 Der ___ (Konrad Adenauer)
28 Deer ___
30 Garage job
32 Like some candles
34 When flowers bloom: Abbr.

36 Crew members
37 "M*A*S*H" co-star
38 Feminizing suffix
40 Attention-getting cry
44 Test sites
46 Handles roughly
48 Linguist Chomsky
50 Relatively cool red giant
51 Remain inactive
52 How actors should appear
54 Jazz's Carmen
56 Drop paper in a box, maybe
57 Coll. major
59 Tex's neighbor
60 Especially
61 It's about 2½ times as high as Vesuvius
64 W.B.A. finales

by Mike Nothnagel

ACROSS

1 Fifth stroke, often
5 Tatter
8 Shoeboy's offering
14 Tony player on "NYPD Blue"
15 Home of the Clearwater Mtns.
16 Not necessarily rejecting
17 Draws
19 Edberg who won two Wimbledons
20 1972 musical with the song "Summer Nights"
22 Actress Graff
23 Ancient Romans' attire
26 Draws
28 Graduate
30 "Isn't ___ bit like you and me?" (Beatles lyric)
31 Retired barrier breaker, for short
32 Law or medicine, e.g.
33 Sole support
34 Weight
35 Awakens
37 Sermonizer in France
41 Tiant in the Red Sox Hall of Fame
42 Angiogram sight
44 Pollen holder
47 Porter, e.g.
48 Pest eradicator
49 Draws
52 Having steam come out the ears, say
53 W.W. II blockade enforcer
54 Old Athenian ally against Persia
56 What fools do, per an adage
58 Draws

62 ___ Green, Scottish town famous for runaway weddings
63 Head lines, in brief?
64 What may ensure the show goes on?
65 Annapolis graduate
66 Gridiron stat.
67 Hightailed it

DOWN

1 By means of
2 "What's the ___?"
3 Middle X, say
4 Draws
5 Rather smelly
6 Attaché attachments
7 Hardly in
8 Like some poles: Abbr.
9 Kind of scanner
10 Female companion in "Doctor Who"
11 Draws
12 Politicians take them
13 Square
18 Papas of "Zorba the Greek"
21 One on it may be out of it
23 Sonora snack
24 "The Good Earth" mother
25 Wise one
27 Board with a couple of seats
29 Villainess in "The Little Mermaid"
33 1961 Elvis hit "___ Latest Flame"
36 Supermodel Cheryl
37 Draws
38 Key letter
39 Harte of fiction
40 Brontë heroine
41 Kind of impression

43 John ___, Doris Day's co-star in "The Pajama Game"
44 Poinsettia's family
45 The Tigers of the Southeastern Conference
46 Draws
48 Took a twisty path
50 Emmy winner Christine
51 It's news in sports
55 Rules, for short
57 A Bobbsey twin
59 Turning point?
60 When day is done, briefly
61 This may be sold by the yard

by Victor Fleming

18

ACROSS

1 In a poem, it "perched upon a bust of Pallas just above my chamber door"
6 Sing like Mel Tormé
10 Use cue cards
14 Slightly ahead
15 Part of a military band
16 ___ dixit
17 Anxious baseball player at the plate?
19 Talk like Daffy
20 Supermarket bagful
21 Great literature it's not
22 Wallpaper and such
23 "Big Sur" writer, 1962
25 Worst in the worst way
27 Sign above a luau buffet?
29 Working factory, e.g.
32 Actress Popplewell of "The Chronicles of Narnia"
33 ___ in victory
34 Hogwarts stick
35 High-school disrupters
37 Big party
38 ___ premium
39 Out of order
40 Broad valleys
41 Land of laughs?
45 Horace who founded the New York Tribune
46 They may be seen on slides
50 Certain resident of Yemen
51 Ready
52 Home of Sault Ste. Marie: Abbr.
53 It may be held at a 39-Down

54 Flood of ideas?
57 Observer
58 Barn young 'un
59 Where to see "bombs bursting"
60 Flat sound
61 One who wants you to put away everything he sets out
62 Two-time "Time" Man of the Year (and a hint to 17-, 27-, 41- and 54-Across)

DOWN

1 1980s craze starter
2 Quickly
3 Campaign target
4 Suffix with insist
5 Preinterview purchase, maybe
6 Lit, as a match
7 Zealot's group
8 Five-spot
9 Contents of some pits
10 Provoke
11 "War and Peace," e.g.
12 Business partner
13 Takes the starch out of
18 Product promoted as having both "beauty" and "brains"
22 Nickelodeon's explorer
24 Newspaper piece
25 Chinese secret society
26 Directs
28 One-named New Age musician
29 Road trip events
30 Popular dates for dates
31 Loser at the dice table
35 Blood
36 Out of whack
37 Actress Dunaway
39 Shop with 53-Across
40 Pays a visit
42 Choir section
43 Duty
44 Harbinger
47 Powdered cleaning agent
48 Hospital procedure, for short
49 Draconian
51 Washed out
54 Abbr. atop some e-mails
55 Cheering word
56 Sea urchin, at a sushi bar

by Samuel A. Donaldson

ACROSS

1 Rock band with the triple-platinum album "High Voltage"
5 Direct sales giant
10 Ins. plan
13 Something sold in half sizes
14 Restraints
15 Orange Free State settler
16 Broken out, in a way
17 Liqueur flavoring
18 Constellation with a music-related name
19 Effects seen down the road
22 Be stingy with
25 Large container
26 Hollywood's Davis
27 ___ fat
28 Type on a computer
30 Peace of mind
31 Bed problem
32 Frame jobs
37 TV series that's now a film franchise
40 Chargers
41 Wall St. takeover
42 Faun, in part
43 Peak performance?
45 Call into question
46 Sought-after object
50 Big inits. in records
51 Popular Art Deco prints
52 Mischief-makers (you'll find seven of them in the answer grid)
55 Spear
56 Russian Literature Nobelist Ivan
57 Darned spot, often
61 Poetry ___
62 Follow, as a tip
63 Sauce maker
64 Scrabble 1-pointer
65 Offering a stark choice
66 Spontaneous skits

DOWN

1 Venom source
2 Curious George, for one
3 Can. or Aust. money
4 Like some black tea
5 Open ___ of worms
6 Legume used to produce sprouts
7 Quills, sometimes
8 Out
9 Nieuwpoort's river
10 Big East basketball powerhouse
11 Polite Parisian's response
12 Deliver a stemwinder
15 Sights at many football games
20 Clip-___
21 Customs
22 Sap sites
23 Banded snake
24 Deadlock
29 Petro-Canada competitor
31 Passable
33 Seafood cocktail ingredient
34 Destroyer hunter
35 Almost win
36 Green and Rogen of comedies
38 Tennyson work
39 Nowhereness
44 Figure out
45 Drive forward
46 See for a second
47 Muscat money
48 Rockefeller Center figure
49 List unit
53 Web site with PowerSellers
54 ___ time
58 Plug's place
59 Immodesty
60 Verb on valentine candy

by Doug Peterson

ACROSS

1 Joshua's companion, in the Old Testament
6 Historic mansion in Newport, R.I., with "the"
10 Stone at a stream crossing
14 Done to death
15 Flood survivor
16 Former currency of Vatican City
17 Curl the hair of
18 Holey things
19 What some use to ply their craft?
20 Some Cubans in Texas?
23 Took a dip
24 Western end of I-190 near I-294
25 Where hot jazz developed?
31 Untighten
32 Untight
33 Have ___ at
36 "The emerald of Europe"
37 "Go, and catch a falling star" poet
38 Put one's foot down
39 Heartbreak
40 International Olympics chief Jacques
41 Up
42 Broadway deli offerings?
44 Japanese immigrant's child
47 Ends
48 20-, 25- and 42-Across, so to speak
54 Without ___ (unsafely)
55 How some receivers go
56 Floated downstream, in a way
58 Wrapper weight
59 Start a hand, maybe
60 Greeting in an inbox
61 "Day Is Dying in the West," for one
62 Heath
63 Zero out

DOWN

1 Part of a price: Abbr.
2 Cunning
3 Ancient dynasty of northern China
4 Pre-Roman Roman
5 Affairs, slangily
6 Buggy field?
7 Wacko
8 Playwright Connelly
9 Division of Islam
10 They often go out on a limb
11 Piece among the crown jewels
12 Unwanted computer message
13 So last week
21 Follow (along)
22 Beverage brand whose logo is two lizards
25 Rowers
26 Purple Heart recipient
27 "Would ___?"
28 River below the Boyoma Falls
29 Silver topper?
30 Practice
33 Measurement with square units
34 Billy, e.g.
35 They may be even, ironically
37 Daily news quote, with "the"
38 Alcohol, slangily
40 Pull back (in)
41 Current measurer
42 Put in order
43 Black bag, maybe
44 Under, to a poet
45 "Uh-uh"
46 Kind of whale
49 Dis
50 Prefix with sphere
51 "I'm ___ you!"
52 Wharton degs.
53 Desiccated
57 Banned pesticide

by Ian Tullis

ACROSS

1 Sounds from Santa
4 Habitually, for short
7 "Men in Black" actor
14 *Settler in a pharmacy
16 Retell
17 Bawl club?
18 Dressed down
19 Some sorority women
20 Actor Jannings
21 *"___ Island"
24 Oodles
28 Tracks
30 Conjecture
33 Crumbs
34 Year in Trajan's reign
35 Emergency lights
36 It's like "-like"
37 *B'way hit beginning in '88
39 "Treasure Island" monogram
40 Sir Richard who cofounded the Spectator
42 Western treaty grp.
43 Nabors role
44 Spilling one's drink at a shindig, for one
46 Neighborhoods in New York and London
47 Italian bone
48 *Where Delta Air Lines is headquartered
50 Dinesen who wrote "Out of Africa"
53 Product once pitched by Pelé
56 Like juicy biographies
59 Some cricketers
60 Bygone McDonald's mascot
61 *Cast a spell over
62 Gently towels off
63 One in a series
64 Directory data: Abbr.

DOWN

1 Peddle
2 ___-Day
3 Ones joining the family
4 Oodles
5 Historic event
6 QBs' scores
7 Hearty steak
8 Gossip's subject
9 Prefix with scope or meter
10 Refrain from singing?
11 Stable particle
12 Interstate sign abbr.
13 "Nightmare ___," 1997 Disney animated series
15 Consternates: Var.
22 Home to some elephants
23 Indy 500 mishap
25 Actress Mary Martin's actor son
26 Opera set in Cyprus
27 The "Working Girl" girl and others
28 San Luis ___
29 Outlooks
31 Corporate money mgrs.
32 German city on the Danube
34 Person who's often sent compliments
37 Wield
38 One way to stand
41 Study for astronomes
43 White, granular powder
45 Annie with a gun
46 Teller
49 ___-dernier (penultimate: Fr.)
51 High-school org.
52 Yank or Ranger
54 The Biggest Little City in the World
55 "Marchers" through the answers to the five starred clues
56 Cough syrup amt.
57 DDT banner
58 Reason for a third serve
59 Little Joe's pa on "Bonanza"

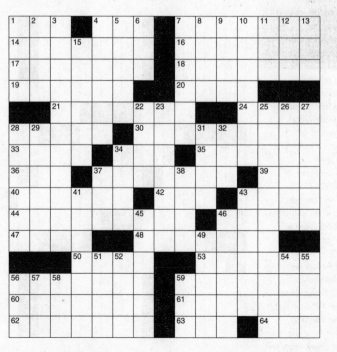

by Patrick Blindauer

22

ACROSS

1 Fruit variety with a sweet-spiced flavor
5 Parents
10 Patron saint of sailors
14 ___ Arena (Kings' home, once)
15 Godspeed
16 Geological range
17 Uruguay and Paraguay
18 Yosemite rock features
19 Money bigwigs, for short
20 So-called "fox fires"
23 Three-time P.G.A. Championship winner
24 Intl. org. dismantled in 1977
25 Penicillin target
29 Infuriated
32 Outdoor cooking spot
35 Recording device
38 Having shipped out
40 Élan
41 "In principio ___ Verbum"
42 Certain lawsuit
45 Tampa-to-Fort Myers dir.
46 Mother ___
47 Kitchen gadget brand
49 Who's creator
52 List in an insurance report, maybe
56 What the ends of 20-, 35- and 42-Across are, collectively
60 ___ Sailer, three-time 1956 skiing gold medalist
61 "See, how she leans her cheek upon her hand!" speaker
62 B.C. neighbor
63 Big area of philanthropy, with "the"
64 "Mi chiamano Mimi" and others
65 Resting place
66 Reassuring words after an accident
67 Big city newspaper desk
68 Car radio mode

DOWN

1 Stock holders
2 Night sky feature
3 Get the point?
4 Longtime NBC Olympics host
5 Wane
6 Repute
7 Represent by drawing
8 Falls (over)
9 "Wake Up Little ___"
10 On every single occasion
11 Take-home?
12 Calls to farmers
13 Carry-___
21 Modern show shower
22 Certain ballroom event
26 European capital
27 Cabinet dept.
28 Penne topper
30 S&L offerings
31 November 4, e.g.
32 A sergeant might ask soldiers to pick it up
33 Española, for one
34 Lambastes
36 Johnny with the 1958 hit "Willie and the Hand Jive"
37 Codger
39 Record follower, at times
43 "Leaving Las Vegas" actress
44 ___ Point Lighthouse, Massachusetts landmark since 1838
48 Detox centers
50 "Hit the road!"
51 Stock holder
53 "I mean it!"
54 Socratic student
55 Desolate
56 R.A.'s place
57 Rule out
58 Parent
59 Blah
60 James Clavell's "___-Pan"

by Chuck Hamilton

ACROSS

1 What the 13 circled things in this puzzle constitute
5 Light from a lantern, say
10 Pound delivery
13 Latin word on a cornerstone
14 20/20, e.g.
15 Max
16 Devices for music lovers
18 This and that
19 TV screen choice: Abbr.
20 Yo-yo
21 A.L. or N.L. Division Series format
23 Off the charts?
25 Like squads in arena football
28 Anatomical duct
29 Eye liners
32 Something that may hold up a train?
35 Guise
37 Prelude to many a kiss
38 Never idle
40 Auto monogram
41 Trifling
43 Bodywide
45 Dashed figs.
46 Donkey Kong, e.g.
47 Fail, as a flick
48 Full coverage?
52 Tool for a driver or painter
55 Crank (up)
56 U.R.L. ender
59 Invitation info
60 "Bad Girl" singer
63 Gofer
64 Actor Hirsch of "Into the Wild"
65 Grp. for court pros
66 Actor known as the King of Cool
67 Baby-sits
68 Barefaced

DOWN

1 ___ Adams, signature on the Declaration of Independence
2 Like calling a woman a "chick," say
3 Having depth
4 Blouse, e.g.
5 Reach
6 Breaks up flights
7 When the French fry?
8 Winged mammoth
9 Wine region where Riesling is made
10 Neighbor of N.M.
11 "Keep dreaming!"
12 Like many office jobs
15 Advil alternative
17 Airline to Chile
22 Bargain hunter's lure
23 Game with a yelled name
24 Spot
25 "Scratch that!"
26 Old PC software
27 Whoops at sea
30 Body layer
31 Welcome
33 Says "My bad!"
34 Deck (out)
35 Some engines
36 Big ring stone, slangily
39 Juvenile, in horse racing
42 Unbelievable
44 H
46 Building with walls for a ceiling
49 Fill a flat again?
50 Rulers like Juan Carlos
51 Actress Mendes of "Hitch"
52 Skinny-dipped
53 In
54 "Through the Looking-Glass" antagonist
56 Greek summit
57 No-good
58 Airborne irritant
61 ___ plate
62 Hike

by Jeremy Newton

24

ACROSS

1 Pioneering 35mm. camera
6 ___ Kong
10 Tactical ballistic missile
14 Get all A's
15 Foreign prince
16 Cannes presentation
17 Kind of bank
18 ___-tiller
19 One-two connector
20 [See circled letters]
23 No. that should be as low as possible
24 Part of a French face
25 Certain Crimeans
26 Cause during Prohibition
28 One caught in a police sting
30 Year Michelangelo began "David"
31 Virginia locale where the C.I.A. is headquartered
33 "The Hound of the Baskervilles" setting
34 [See circled letters]
38 Insincere talk
39 "That's a lie!," e.g.
40 "___, what eyes hath Love put in my head": Shak.
41 Cowherd's aid
43 Supermodel Bündchen
47 Sound in a Bobby Darin song title
49 ___ esprit
50 10 on a 10-point scale, e.g.
51 [See circled letters]
55 Arm part
56 "Time ___" (bygone sci-fi series)
57 A sheriff may be seen in it
58 Gather
59 Sun block
60 Take forcibly
61 To be overseas
62 P.M. known as the Iron Lady
63 Exterminators' targets

DOWN

1 Richard ___, director of "Help!" and "A Hard Day's Night"
2 Run out
3 Martian feature
4 Supreme Court writ, familiarly
5 Output from Benjamin Franklin's press
6 National alternative
7 Autobiographical novel of 1847
8 Time on a marquee
9 Business goal
10 Meager
11 Gum choice
12 Victor of an upset
13 It may follow a name and address
21 Bass relative
22 McKellen who played Gandalf
27 Let out
28 Gabbed
29 Put ___ act
32 Inner: Prefix
33 Wire measures
34 Flier
35 Quick laugh
36 Star of Orion
37 Clinch, as a victory
38 Something you might go to a party in
41 Wash. winter hours
42 Cadence
44 Conveys feelings
45 Least convincing
46 Applies
48 Steaming
49 Round person?
52 "Dies ___"
53 "Hogan's Heroes" figure
54 Like a Liberty gold coin

by Allan E. Parrish

ACROSS

1 Tobias ___, author of "This Boy's Life"
6 Sound of a sax
10 Fish that can detect ultrasound
14 Director Kurosawa
15 Kind of sax
16 Spinner for the Spinners
17 Start of a quote by economist Allan Meltzer
19 Come ___
20 First mate's superior, informally
21 Sanded, e.g.
23 Quote, part 2
26 Eastern queen
27 See 59-Across
28 Consoling words
30 Some monitors, for short
31 Game pieces
34 Like most Olympic gymnasts
37 Dressy accessories
39 "Either plagiarism or revolution," according to Gauguin
40 Choice that avoids choosing
42 "___ bleu!"
43 Occasion to say goodbye
46 Ray who founded McDonald's
47 Quote, part 3
51 One who believes humans descended from extraterrestrials
52 20-Across's crew
53 Image in the Notre Dame de Paris
54 End of the quote
59 With 27-Across, it collapsed in 2008
60 Tribe speaking Chiwere
61 Pact since 1993
62 Web addresses
63 Constellation between Cygnus and Hercules
64 I.R.A. option

DOWN

1 Extra in "I Was a Male War Bride"
2 Volga feeder
3 Edge
4 Heat producer
5 Palestinian group
6 Waldorf salad ingredient
7 Noted ring leader
8 "Honest to goodness!"
9 Winning coach of the first two Super Bowls
10 Bars of a sort
11 Mahatma Gandhi, for one
12 Pursuing
13 Device also called a rectifier
18 Blood type, for short
22 Pours 23-Down on
23 See 22-Down
24 Map box
25 ___ no.
26 Singer Coolidge
29 Tokyo theater performance
31 Prefix with surgery
32 2005 documentary subtitled "The Smartest Guys in the Room"
33 Fraction of an instant: Abbr.
35 Off-base?
36 Forever and a day
38 Commonwealth member beginning in 1947
41 Charlemagne ruled it: Abbr.
43 Manicurists
44 1950s tennis champion Gibson
45 Chinese dynasty a thousand years ago
47 Pitcher Hideki ___
48 More there?
49 Corporate department
50 Menial worker
55 Prominence
56 West Coast airport inits.
57 Cousin ___ of "The Addams Family"
58 Not, to a Scot

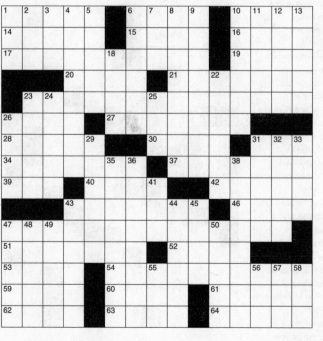

by Pete Muller

ACROSS

1. Attain new heights
6. Chile's ___ de Pascua
10. Castaway's clothing
14. Rapids transit?
15. Established
17. Troubadours carried them
18. Country that has won the most Cricket World Cups
19. Poetic preposition
20. Parcel of land
22. Export of 18-Across
23. Day trader's wish
25. He brings people together
26. Abound
27. Stand and deliver
29. Between
31. Zero ___
32. King in I Kings
36. Dynasty in which Confucianism became dominant
37. Break away
39. Attained new heights
40. Jump that may be doubled
42. "I couldn't ___!"
44. Accelerate
45. Org. with a National Historic Landmark building in lower Manhattan
46. Ex-senator Sam
47. Op-ed piece
49. Bellyache
51. Danger for small craft
52. Contemporary of Kepler
54. Formula formulators
58. Actor Shore
59. Prince ___, Eddie Murphy's role in "Coming to America"
60. Step on it
61. Location of two of the classical Seven Wonders

63. Domicile
65. Spicy biscuit served at English teas
66. Sole pattern
67. Cannonball Adderley's "Somethin' ___"
68. Dr. ___, 1990s TV therapist
69. Before sunrise

DOWN

1. Symbol seen on viola music
2. 1944 film noir by Preminger
3. Digestive system parts with recycling?
4. Baseball's Berg
5. Most promising options with recycling?
6. Son of Sarah
7. Took a risk with recycling?
8. Caboose's place
9. Upscale office décor
10. Come back with recycling?
11. Two-time loser to Ike
12. Craft union of old
13. Rest spots
16. Freshwater catch
21. Ingredient in a Bahama Mama
24. La. neighbor
25. Victorian gents' accessories
28. "The Age of Bronze" artist
29. Comparative follower
30. Like Stilton cheese
31. Put on a winter coat?
33. Livery blacksmith with recycling?
34. Like pirates
35. Large group

38. Naively optimistic Muppet
41. Imposition on drinking with recycling?
43. Sporting colleague with recycling?
48. Kind of run
50. Have common ends, in a way
51. Lilliputian
52. So-called "king of herbs"
53. Mayan pyramids, e.g.
55. Enterprise rival
56. Like some currents
57. Poorly kept
58. Ask for by name
59. Ballerina Pavlova
62. Discommode
64. Sports ___

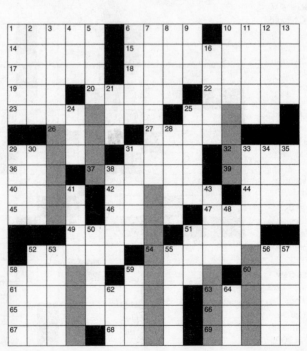

by Patrick Berry

ACROSS

1 Denver-to-Santa Fe dir.
4 Loads
9 French greeting
14 E.P.A. pollution meas.
15 Like Rembrandt
16 Magyar : Hungarian :: Gaeilge : ___
17 Dull shade
18 Bridge authority
20 With intensity
22 Yahoo! competitor
23 River of Saxony
24 Typical postcard attractions
26 Penpoint
27 Soup or salad ingredient
30 '60s leftist grp.
31 Medicated candy
36 Victory, Viennese-style
37 Greek war goddess
38 Comparatively quick communication
43 Intellectual conclusion?
45 Deform
46 Many a corp. hire
47 Joltin' Joe
50 Actor Tamiroff
51 It lies beneath Wayne Manor
53 Regain consciousness
55 Verizon reference
58 Implement with a collar
59 Infatuation
60 "You win"
61 DHL rival
62 So-called Hermit Kingdom of old
63 & 64 Words that can precede the starts of 18-, 31-, 38- and 55-Across

DOWN

1 Most blue
2 Silence
3 Reception amenity
4 Like shipping and handling, typically: Abbr.
5 First of a Disney trio
6 Series finale?: Abbr.
7 "Egad!"
8 Nokia offering
9 Examines, as evidence
10 Home of Snowflake, which, ironically, gets very little snow: Abbr.
11 Marriage requirement
12 Cyberhandle
13 Hurts like heck
19 Small number
21 Hastert's successor as speaker of the House
24 One end of the Moscow Canal
25 Daughter of Cadmus
28 Wilderness home
29 Big-ticket ___
32 Hit 1983 pseudo-documentary
33 Big pictures: Abbr.
34 Louis and Carrie
35 Setting for the 51-Across
38 Dabbler
39 "___ Man," top 10 hit of 1967
40 Pizza order, frequently
41 "Everybody loves somebody sometime," for Dean Martin
42 Factor in sentencing
43 Announcement after being away
44 Italian restaurant chain
47 Russian country house
48 ___ Andric, 1961 Literature Nobelist
49 Kit carrier
52 Costco quantity
53 Hombre's home
54 It's to the left of #
56 Right-angled joint
57 First name in slapstick

by Barry C. Silk

ACROSS

1 Part of a pay-as-you-go plan?
6 She'll "always have Paris"
10 Has obligations
14 Japanese brew
15 "Mighty" things
16 District in Hawaii
17 2008 Olympics tennis champion Dementieva
18 Meander, as a road
20 That over there
21 Author of "Something Wicked This Way Comes"
23 Inventor depicted in "The Prestige"
25 Long ago
26 Hinged apparatus
29 Walks down the aisle
31 Supplicate
33 Reverses course
37 Off-color
38 "Zounds!"
39 Like some calls left on answering machines
42 Diet
43 Leveler
45 Petrify
47 Cub raiser
50 M.P.'s concern
51 Music producer Brian
52 Walked off with
54 NATO member since 1982
57 Comparatively honest
59 Bopper
61 Crucial moment
64 1836 siege site, with "the"
66 Cadre, e.g.
67 "The Martha ___ Show" of 1950s TV
68 Scene of Hercules' first labor
69 Gang members
70 Comment about a loss
71 Upset

DOWN

1 Fully equipped and ready to go
2 Kitchen light
3 Emmy and Tony nominee Ryan
4 Blood
5 Equips
6 Tiny bit
7 "___ Miss Clawdy" (#1 R&B hit of 1952)
8 Winter vehicle
9 Guarantee
10 "Go ahead!"
11 Korean money
12 Doomsday, with "the"
13 Roman god of agriculture
19 Lock with no key?
22 Airport installation
24 Where the Riksdag meets
26 Kraft Foods brand
27 Be a cast member of
28 Cry from someone who's been aggrieved
30 Seek restitution, perhaps
32 Calif. barrio setting
33 Old country-and-western star ___ Travis
34 Over
35 Instrument unlikely to be heard at Carnegie Hall
36 1965 #1 hit by the Byrds
40 H
41 Search for water, in a way
44 Fix, as a pool cue
46 Aida, for one
48 Neighbor of Arizona
49 Tea, e.g.
53 Mount ___, second-highest peak in Africa
55 Part of Caesar's boast
56 Christener
57 Company leaders: Abbr.
58 G.P.S. output: Abbr.
60 Perfectly
61 Eventually appear
62 ___ bit
63 Zip
65 Book after Exod.

by Jim Hilger

ACROSS

1 "Numb3rs" airer
4 Bearded
9 In ___ (quickly)
14 Where to go in Greenwich?
15 It may be tragic
16 They start in the middle
17 Keeper of confidential information
20 Noodle
21 Sneaking
22 Wrongs
23 The last King Edward of England
25 "O terra, addio," e.g.
26 Like a keeper of confidential information
32 Title role for Valentino
33 ___ Majesty
34 Fruit used in English jelly
35 Slippery one
36 Subject of Exodus 20:10
40 "Can't fool me!"
41 ___ fides (bad faith)
43 Cause of a scare
44 Daisylike flower
46 With 60-Across, what a keeper of confidential information might say
50 Leeway
51 Unoccupied
52 Scammer's skill
55 Certain qualifications
56 Djinn's home in a popular tale
60 See 46-Across
63 Bring out
64 Buck for a song?
65 Slippery one?
66 Harnesses
67 Like the sun
68 Davy Jones's locker, with "the"

DOWN

1 Listing in a high-school yearbook
2 Something to pick
3 Part of many a drink order
4 Bearer of cones
5 Inverse trig function
6 "Enough!"
7 Part of a famous septet
8 Alter, in a way
9 With French, one of two official languages of Chad
10 Porsche alternatives
11 Day of destiny
12 Numismatist's classification
13 They may be thrown
18 Poetic coda
19 Most prized, often
24 Gets to
25 Part of a famous septet
26 Stack of papers
27 "___ never!"
28 "Yippee!"
29 Lift up
30 Singer/songwriter Leonard
31 Sophomores, e.g.
32 Rest stop sight
37 Wear away, as a metallic surface
38 Factor in a wine rating
39 Bad feeling?
42 Tranquil
45 Hard case
47 Tapenade ingredients
48 Out of tune
49 Bearish
52 Legislature
53 Icelandic volume
54 Confidant
55 Home of Private Ryan in "Saving Private Ryan"
57 First side to vote
58 Spicy chocolate sauce
59 Big brand in athletic footwear
61 Rocky peak
62 Cause of tripping?

by Michael Vuolo

ACROSS

1 Choker component
6 Music pioneered by Byron Lee and the Dragonaires
9 ___ Secretary
14 Rummage
15 Suffer
16 Bygone Olds
17 Sorkin who created "The West Wing"
18 Section in a record store
20 Chestnut-colored mustang offspring?
22 Its coat of arms includes a vicuña
23 "Rule, Britannia" composer Thomas
24 Nuts
27 Like the space around a first-class seat, say
29 Con
33 Pitcher Hideo Nomo's birthplace
35 "No ___" ("Beats me")
37 Ripen
38 Main dedicatee of an Austin cathedral?
42 "Talk to ___," Pedro Almodóvar film
43 Time-honored name?
44 Food processor setting
45 Torpedoed
47 David ___, founder of the Libertarian Party
50 A.A.A. jobs
51 ___ were
53 Brick maker
55 Hefty invoice for boots and spurs?
62 On the fence
63 Dashboard item
64 Emasculate
65 Embarrassed, perhaps
66 Last name of Kipling's Kim
67 Fresh
68 ___ Balls (snack cakes)
69 Masters champ of 1949, 1952 and 1954

DOWN

1 Grouch
2 Epithet that's an anagram of 60-Down
3 Big do
4 Snail
5 Pasta salad ingredient
6 Pelvic bone
7 Overseas shipping unit
8 Star of Broadway's "QED," 2001–02
9 Brick placer
10 Walker, Cooper and others
11 Art ___
12 Asia's ___ Sea
13 Shed
19 Present for viewing . . . or prevent from being viewed
21 Bust holder
24 Ness and Tay
25 Dublin-born film star Milo
26 ___ terrier
28 Dot
30 The City of a Thousand Minarets
31 Predecessor of Ford
32 Doles (out)
34 Org. founded by Samuel Gompers
36 Saharan viper
39 Garb for Robin Hood and his band
40 Trips through rain forests, maybe
41 Famously fast route
46 Home of Fort Scott National Historic Site
48 Light ratio in astronomy
49 Prefix with romantic
52 Like some silences
54 Spinners
55 Prey for lions
56 College in New Rochelle, N.Y.
57 Mall conveniences
58 Cousin of a treecreeper
59 Family name suffix in taxonomy
60 Money that's an anagram of 2-Down
61 Dishwasherful

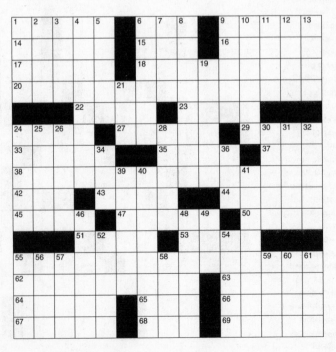

by Eric Tentarelli

ACROSS

1 Brisk pace
5 Satirist who wrote jokes for J.F.K.
9 Hardly getting along
14 Sight blocker
15 Oil of ___
16 Who opposed George Washington for president in 1792
17 Independent
19 Justin Timberlake's former band
20 Do a marathon in Egypt?
22 Not rejecting out of hand
23 Leave open-mouthed
24 Señor chaser?
27 Close to the hour
30 Surround
32 Bro, say
35 Some kind of a nut
37 Goes all out at an audition for a sax great?
41 Suddenly
42 Formerly named
43 Irish ___
44 Take care of one's taxes sans paper
48 Inside look, for short?
49 Drivel
51 "___ Brasco" (1997 Pacino/ Depp film)
55 Top-secret carpentry tool?
59 Mend, as a torn seam
61 Add up
62 It often has a ring in the middle
63 Yours, overseas
64 Yakutsk's river
65 Intoxicating
66 Dermatologist's concern
67 D-Day vessels: Abbr.

DOWN

1 Complete, for short
2 Accumulated
3 O₃
4 One paying for staying
5 "Already?"
6 Diamond family name
7 Best Supporting Actress for "Cactus Flower," 1969
8 Carter who played Wonder Woman
9 Dirty campaign technique
10 Mr. Potato Head piece
11 Band whose 1994 song "I'll Make Love to You" was #1 for 14 weeks
12 Novelist Packer or Patchett
13 Read a New Book Mo.
18 Art Deco designer
21 Worry about, in slang
25 Shopworn
26 Stunned, after "in"
28 Gulf of ___
29 TV's "Fawlty Towers," for one
31 Squirting flower or dribble glass
32 Tic
33 More wonderful, to a hip-hopper
34 Part of Poland's border
36 Certain scale start
38 China's Sun ___-sen
39 Leave for a bit
40 Rings at Jewish weddings?
45 "Hurray for me!"
46 Co-founder of MGM
47 Ultimate goal
50 "Nonsense!"
52 Rear end, anatomically
53 Birth cert., e.g.
54 Pound and Stone
56 Furnish
57 Smidgen
58 "Dona ___ and Her Two Husbands"
59 Bit of cheer?
60 "___ the bat hath flown / His cloister'd flight . . .": Macbeth

by Alan Arbesfeld

ACROSS

1 Weakens
6 Chink in the armor, say
10 Book after Joel
14 The Sorbonne, for one
15 Jot
16 It's in a pickle
17 Supermodels?
19 Just
20 Continued drama
21 Caboose, e.g.
23 Make one to one, perhaps
24 One who fattens up cattle?
28 Razz
31 Jot
32 Flapper accessory
33 Legal org.
34 Narnia's Aslan, e.g.
35 Duke's quarters?
37 Bit of advice from a tennis coach?
41 Bridge supports
42 Work on the street
43 Be prostrate
44 Bad-mouth
45 Monet's "Done!"
46 Nabors role
47 45s from Count Basie and Benny Goodman?
51 ___ trick
52 Monet work
53 Congregation member
57 Final ___
59 From gentle to steep for some playground equipment?
62 Move, in Realtor-speak
63 Pounds, informally
64 Spasm
65 Run in place

66 Pupil of Miss Crump, on TV
67 Much-debated school subject, for short

DOWN

1 Come clean, with "up"
2 Hurt
3 One can be shown to you
4 Nancy's aunt in Nancy Drew mysteries
5 Go after
6 Working out just fine?
7 Mauna ___
8 Still
9 "That ___ so bad"
10 Fuss
11 Sage and thyme are in it

12 N.F.L. Hall-of-Famer Matson
13 More devious
18 Not too quick
22 "Porgy" novelist ___ Heyward
25 Chinese dynasty lasting eight centuries
26 Cartel leader
27 Kids' snow construction
28 See 45-Down
29 Disbeliever's comment
30 Stripped
34 "Come on!"
35 Coupe ___
36 Potter's purchase
38 Target for Dracula
39 The Jets, e.g.
40 Once called

45 Standard 28-Down purchase
46 The id is in it
47 Sci-fi novelist ___ S. Tepper
48 Like some floors and legs
49 R&B singer with the hit "Thong Song"
50 Bridge positions
54 Last name in comedy
55 Healing balm
56 Exigency
58 Curly whacker
60 Only Super Bowl won by the Jets
61 34th U.S. pres.

by Joe DiPietro

ACROSS

1 Irish interjection
8 Part of some resort names: Abbr.
11 One way to get something down
14 The Black Stallion, e.g.
15 Paul Anka hit that made it to #19
17 & 18 "J'ai Deux Amours" singer
19 Whitish
20 Extended vacationers may take them
21 Goes back
25 Pulitzer-winning biographer Leon
26 & 29 Tangerine
33 Nickname preceder
34 "One Song Glory" musical
36 Rice pad
37 U.S.N. clerk: Abbr.
38 Burglary . . . or a hint to 17/18-, 26/29-, 47/51- and 62/63-Across
42 Viral inflammation, informally
43 Sailor's saint
45 Paradoxical fellow
46 12-time baseball All-Star
47 & 51 Wet-day wish
53 Crush
54 Literary pen name
55 Chinese chicken flavorers
58 Gracile
62 & 63 Temporary setback
66 Baby shower attendees, often
67 Can't-miss proposition
68 "Shame on you!"
69 Lush
70 Gets together

DOWN

1 Mexican peninsula
2 One taking a bow?
3 Nasty wound
4 Minded
5 It may be written in stone
6 Rallying cry?
7 What causes Fred to be fired?
8 Longtime breath freshener
9 Fake
10 Person holding things up?
11 Chow alternative
12 Play ___ (do some tennis)
13 Rocky peaks
16 "The ___ of Reading Gaol" (Wilde poem)
22 Zinger
23 Word before Rabbit or Fox
24 Trig ratio
26 Early film executive
27 "The Jungle Book" wolf
28 She renamed herself Mara, in Scripture
30 Slangy negative
31 Scacchi of "Presumed Innocent"
32 Drain
35 Looney Tunes nickname
39 Grasps
40 Actress Swenson of "Benson"
41 Hiding place
44 Cloverleaf component
48 Relatives of cha-cha-chas
49 Danny of "Ruby"
50 Be emphatic
52 Where shopping carts are pushed
55 Mil. rank
56 Some guesses, for short
57 Be ill-humored
59 High balls?
60 Summer cooler
61 Trading places: Abbr.
63 Code crackers' org.
64 Bazooka, e.g.
65 Word with sports or training

by Patrick Blindauer

34

ACROSS

1. Schmo
5. Trash cans and such
10. Walking encyclopedia
14. "How did ___ this happen?"
15. Opposite of someways
16. Alto lead-in?
17. Paris's ___ de Lyon
18. Benjamin
19. Wood alternative
20. Split
23. Refrain from singing in kindergarten?
24. Picketer's sign
28. Zing
29. Chinese dollar
33. All over
34. 1990s war site
36. ___ feuilletée (puff pastry)
37. Primitive trophies . . . or a hint to this puzzle's theme
41. Karmann ___ (old Volkswagen)
42. Genuine
43. Alternative rock band with four platinum albums
46. Repair shop figs.
47. Cry out loud
50. Conformation defect in a horse
52. Words on a Wonderland cake
54. Traffic sign that indicates a possible temporary road closure
58. Deal preceder
61. Cause for pulling over
62. Where Samson defeated the Philistines
63. Lawless role
64. Managing, with "out"
65. Zest
66. Front
67. Go from one number to another
68. 100 18-Acrosses

DOWN

1. Macrocephalic
2. Sainted king known as "the Fat"
3. Numbers in the thousands?
4. "S.N.L." alum
5. Creep
6. Gelato holder
7. "Pick me! I know the answer!"
8. Angry diner's decision
9. Egoist
10. Like a bishop's authority
11. Elongated fish
12. Day-___
13. One way to meet
21. "Happy birthday" follower
22. Back muscle, for short
25. Slightly
26. Fails to keep
27. It's barely passing
30. Seal's org.
31. "My Way" songwriter
32. Eleanor Roosevelt, to Teddy
34. Unable to think at all
35. Things with antennas
37. "Rich Man, Poor Man" novelist, 1970
38. Lie low
39. Wickiup, for one
40. Lightened
41. Test for M.A. seekers
44. Done, to Donne
45. Nut jobs
47. English essayist Richard
48. Certain Nebraska native
49. Lady Jane Grey's fate
51. ___-Mart
53. Shoelace tip
55. Ship part
56. Bausch & Lomb lens-care product
57. Playwright William
58. Chopping part of a chopper
59. French word in some bios
60. Former TV inits.

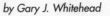

by Gary J. Whitehead

ACROSS

1 Suffix with social
4 Best in mental combat
10 Some rain gear
14 Hold one's ___
15 Time magazine's 2007 Invention of the Year
16 Jacques Cousteau's middle name
17 See 66-Across
20 Cockpit datum
21 Bridge declaration
22 They're inserted in locks
23 City on the Nile
25 See 66-Across
31 Influential Greek physician
32 1/100 of a krone
33 Roof projection
34 Sch. with a Providence campus
35 See 66-Across
39 Ringo's drummer son
40 Plunders
42 Some eggs
43 Products once pitched by U2 and Eminem
45 See 66-Across
49 Basilica part
50 Riga resident
51 Start of Caesar's boast
54 Texas panhandle city
58 See 66-Across
61 Related
62 Soldiers may be on it
63 Abbr. in French mail
64 TV heroine who wielded a chakram as a weapon
65 Sixth graders, e.g.
66 Word defined by 17-, 25-, 35-, 45- and 58-Across

DOWN

1 Seat of Allen County, Kan.
2 Deux : France :: ___ : Germany
3 Technician: Abbr.
4 Artist's application
5 Amphetamines, e.g.
6 Separate the wheat from the chaff
7 Golf club
8 Like Beethoven's Sixth Symphony
9 Place to start a hole
10 News Corporation acquisition of 2005
11 New Balance competitor
12 Business honchos
13 I.R.S. data: Abbr.
18 In harmony
19 Tag info
23 Greek restaurant offering
24 Logical introduction?
25 Captain of industry
26 Out
27 Hole-making tool
28 Shadow remover
29 Duck
30 Mice might elicit them
31 Wise guy
36 Pet sounds
37 The Swiss Guards guard him
38 Cold northerly winds of southern France
41 Endurance
44 "___ down!" ("Drop the gun!")
46 Crude letters?
47 "Get Shorty" novelist ___ Leonard
48 George who directed "Miracle on 34th Street"
51 Big film shower
52 Salad veggie
53 Q ___ queen
54 Chip without dip?
55 An arm or a leg
56 ___ Linda, Calif.
57 Humdinger
59 Fitting
60 Some postgraduate study

by Barry C. Silk

ACROSS

1 Accomplish lots of things
6 Not fitting
11 Year St. Pius I died
14 Sister of Clio
15 Subject of the 2007 documentary "An Unreasonable Man"
16 "Norma ___"
17 Belief
18 Actor who received a 7-Down (1998, 2002, 2005–06, 2009)
20 Popular breath mint
22 Bovine in old ads
23 ___ material (sturdy fabric)
25 More red, maybe
28 Field in which things are looking up?: Abbr.
29 Orient
30 Singer/songwriter who received a 7-Down (2002, 2004–06, 2008, 2011, 2013)
32 Some jazz combos
34 One with a long face?
35 Hot tub
36 Singer who received a 7-Down (2003)
39 Tofu source
42 Moviemaking lamp
43 Pigment used in drawing
45 Singer/actress who received a 7-Down (1996–2002)
50 Difficult sort
51 Extract from a French bean?
52 Party list
53 Terrier type
54 From the top
56 "Steamboat ___," first Mickey Mouse cartoon
58 Comedian who received a 7-Down (2003–06)
61 Amalgam, e.g.
64 One-dimensional: Abbr.
65 Bob Cratchit's occupation
66 To a great extent
67 Switch positions
68 "It takes all ___"
69 Benders?

DOWN

1 Acquire
2 It's found in veins
3 Singer who received a 7-Down (2005, 2009, 2011)
4 Eroded
5 Drillers' org.?
6 Next to Connecticut Avenue, say, on a Monopoly board
7 Annual entertainment honor
8 Navy chief: Abbr.
9 Bank of China Tower architect
10 Logician's drawing
11 Piece of equipment used in a national sport of Canada
12 Looseness
13 Annoying types
19 Bit of snow
21 Song syllable
23 Spurts from fountains
24 O.K. Corral fighter
26 Sch. course with graphs
27 Comedy standout
31 Unchanged
33 Hacienda room
37 Letter start
38 Achilles' weakness
39 Director who received a 7-Down (2007)
40 Like some hair
41 Columbia rival
42 Funnyman Robert
44 Fraternity letter
45 Spanish devil
46 Enter cautiously
47 Gets to know
48 Boonies
49 Sea slitherer
55 Small cut
57 Tall and thin
59 Student at 41-Down
60 Door sign
62 Low digit
63 Football stat: Abbr.

by David J. Kahn

ACROSS

1 "Slumdog Millionaire" locale
5 Find fault
9 Old auto control
14 Move to solid food
15 Scene of classic flooding
16 The Four Seasons, e.g.
17 Influential work by 28-Across, familiarly
20 Bygone leader with a goatee
21 Bit
22 Health ___
23 Dastard
26 Where to see 20th Century Fox studios
28 Notable born 2/12/1809
33 Grp. founded in Jerusalem
34 Part of a knave's loot, in a rhyme
35 1970s Big Apple mayor
36 Sony brand
38 Cheese and crackers, maybe
41 Some
42 Great Lakes fish
44 Tills, in a way
46 Excess
47 Notable born 2/12/1809
51 Role played by 52-Across in "The Story of Mankind"
52 See 51-Across
53 Signs off on
56 Lake Thun's river
58 Absinthe flavor
61 47-Across led it
65 What almost always goes for a buck?
66 2004 Brad Pitt film
67 Tinware art
68 Tour stops
69 End of a phonetic alphabet
70 Genesis grandson

DOWN

1 Object of a hunt, maybe
2 "Runaway Bride" co-star, 1999
3 Drought easer
4 Chest pain
5 Atlanta's ___ Center
6 "A Rainy Night in ___" (1946 hit)
7 European sports car, informally
8 Rouse
9 Beaker site, for short
10 Ad ___
11 Bluesman Rush
12 Not go bad
13 Old-time gossip queen Maxwell
18 Like neon
19 Place for a lily
24 "___ the day!" (Shakespearean exclamation)
25 "Can't Help Lovin' Dat Man" composer
27 Quarter
28 Scale
29 "60 Minutes" correspondent starting in 1991
30 Kitchen appliance
31 "Er . . . uh . . ."
32 Slender amphibian
33 "Qué ___?"
37 Singer Jackson with more than 20 #1 country hits
39 Stamp purchase
40 Numbers game
43 Kindergarten learning
45 Go at it
48 Salty inland ___ Sea
49 St. ___, Switzerland
50 Flowery
53 Christmas tree ornaments, typically
54 R&B singer Hilson
55 Descry
57 Literally, "raw"
59 1944 battle site
60 Checks out
62 "___ Saison en Enfer"
63 Comcast alternative
64 Home of the Stern School of Business: Abbr.

by Gary and Stephen Kennedy

ACROSS

1 One of the Untouchables
5 Disney's "___ and the Detectives"
9 "That's great . . . not!"
14 Ryan of "Star Trek: Voyager"
15 Film character who says "Named must your fear be before banish it you can"
16 It's good for Juan
17 School ___
18 What might have the heading "Collectibles" or "Toys & Hobbies"?
20 Words with innocence or consent
22 Confused responses
23 Optimistic scan at the dentist's?
26 Not recorded
30 Boomer's kid
31 Org. in the Bourne series
32 Conjured up
34 Story of Ali Baba?
37 Many truckers
40 One may be caught in it
41 Sycophant
42 Transmits a message to Pancho and pals?
45 Pressing
46 Naut. heading
47 Letters on some churches
50 Scrabble 10-pointers
51 Amazes a horror film director?
55 Bond villain in "Moonraker"
56 Starters and more
57 Old street cry, or what's in 18-, 23-, 34-, 42- and 51-Across?

63 Bone meaning "elbow" in Latin
64 "Sorry, I did it"
65 A seeming eternity
66 Sale caveat
67 Conductor noted for wearing turtlenecks
68 Unfortunate date ending
69 Dickens's Mr. Pecksniff

DOWN

1 Marshalls competitor
2 Thin, overseas
3 Amount of debt, old-style
4 "I Am Spock" autobiographer
5 Socket filler
6 Kind of scene
7 Home of the City of Rocks National Reserve
8 Easy two points
9 They have bows
10 Ancient pillager
11 President Bartlet on "The West Wing"
12 "Wedding Album" recording artist
13 "That hurt!"
19 Prop on "The Price Is Right"
21 Pay strict attention to
24 Center of holiday decorations
25 Speak in Spanish
26 Racecar adornments
27 Furniture chain
28 Deal in
29 Swirl
33 Nay sayers
34 Essays
35 Second part of a three-part command
36 Dortmund denials

37 "Volver" actress, 2006
38 Not decent
39 Advantage
43 Unsettling look
44 Health supplement store
47 Tear off forcefully
48 Be serious
49 Long hyphen
52 Becomes fuller
53 Honor
54 Water colors
55 Precursor to Surrealism
57 Rock genre
58 Series finale
59 ?, on a sched.
60 Not even rare
61 Code carrier
62 "Poor venomous fool," to Shakespeare

by Kevin G. Der

ACROSS

- **1** Toastmaster's offering
- **5** Worked regularly at
- **10** Home of Ensenada, informally
- **14** "The ___ of Frankenstein" (Peter Cushing film)
- **15** Poet Federico García ___
- **16** Acct. ___
- **17** Delft, e.g.
- **18** "Conversation is ___ in which a man has all mankind for his competitors": Ralph Waldo Emerson
- **19** "Hard ___!" (captain's order)
- **20** Residence
- **23** Some music on the Warped Tour
- **24** "___ see!"
- **25** It has to be asked
- **34** Troubled
- **35** Like Petruchio's wench in "The Taming of the Shrew"
- **36** Middle year of Nero's reign
- **37** Santa's reindeer, e.g.
- **38** Common origami figures
- **39** Ask for
- **40** ___ de coeur
- **41** Clean, in a way
- **42** Consumer electronics giant
- **43** Alumni weekend V.I.P.
- **46** 1961 Top 10 hit "Hello Mary ___"
- **47** Texans' grp.
- **48** Many Haydn compositions
- **56** It comes from Mars
- **57** Casts
- **58** Firm honcho
- **60** Centers of activity
- **61** Finnish architect Alvar ___
- **62** Ambiance
- **63** Something in the air
- **64** Words repeated after "O Absalom" in the Bible
- **65** Occurrence in the moon's first quarter

DOWN

- **1** Wandering ___
- **2** Eyeglass lens shape
- **3** ___ Davis, "A Girl Like Me" documentarian
- **4** Matinee showing time, maybe
- **5** Have in mind
- **6** Pants spec
- **7** Modern home of the ancient Akkadian empire
- **8** It's similar to cream
- **9** Records for computer processing
- **10** "Vamoose!"
- **11** Part of a wheelset
- **12** Raspberry
- **13** Reno's AAA baseball team
- **21** "You're looking at your guy!"
- **22** Upbeat
- **25** Bake sale display
- **26** "In ___" (1993 #1 album)
- **27** Adjust, as a satellite dish
- **28** Twilight, old-style
- **29** Somewhat
- **30** Old hwy. from Detroit to Seattle
- **31** "The L Word" creator/producer Chaiken
- **32** False sunflower
- **33** Coolpix camera maker
- **38** Closed carriage with the driver outside in front
- **39** Its home is on the range
- **41** Capital subj.
- **42** Carpet meas.
- **44** Alchemist's concoction
- **45** She played Mrs. Miniver in "Mrs. Miniver"
- **48** French town of W.W. II
- **49** Lacking depth
- **50** Opposite of pobre
- **51** Unloading site
- **52** They may be bookmarked
- **53** Certain castrato
- **54** Legitimate
- **55** "Buona ___"
- **59** Delete in one quick stroke

by Brendan Emmett Quigley

ACROSS

1 Great Bear Lake locale
7 Blacken
13 Basic pool exercise
14 Lover of Aida
15 Word of warning
16 Potent pitcherfuls
17 Out of action
19 Cold weather wear
22 ___-majesté
23 3-D camera maker
27 Coconut yield?
28 Suckling site
29 Sensitive
30 Put out
32 Rocket first tested in 1957
33 With 16-Down, annual March event
36 Title woman in a Jim Carrey movie
37 Gracious introduction?
39 Schlep
40 Ridged material
42 Certain domino number
43 "What ___?"
44 Learn a lot quickly
45 Fishing tool
46 Big job for a driller
49 It may be revealed by a tree
52 Bingeing
56 Jim Palmer and teammates
57 Fall away
58 Squinted (at)
59 Childish answer

DOWN

1 Ear part
2 Hydrocarbon suffix
3 Unheard of
4 Setting for much of the 33-Across/16-Down
5 "Beavis and Butthead" spinoff
6 Made like
7 Tony- and Emmy-winning actress Blythe
8 Beat by a point or two
9 What the Athabaskan word for the beginning of 33-Across means
10 Friend of 24-Down
11 Start of an apology
12 Cousin of -enne
14 Cultivate
16 See 33-Across
18 Like some statesmen
19 Representation of a budget, often
20 Fleet person
21 Circulation concern
24 "The School for Wives" playwright
25 Part of the Uzbekistan border

26 Choice marks?
28 Actress Hagen
31 Got down
32 Dull finish?
34 Sermon subject
35 It may provide one's sole support
36 Knock off
38 Six-Day War participant: Abbr.
40 Picked up a point or two
41 Some lithographs
45 More moderate
47 Eye
48 Bayes who sang and co-wrote "Shine On, Harvest Moon"
49 Jump off the page
50 "___ I let fall the windows of mine eyes": Shak.

51 Bite the dust
53 A.F.C. East player
54 Bother
55 ___ Metro (bygone car)

by David J. Kahn

ACROSS

1 Result of some oil deposits
5 X
11 Drain
14 Certain cable, informally
15 Provincial capital in NW Spain
16 Pres. initials
17 Classic Cadillacs
19 Cry when seeing something for the first time
20 Positive aspects
21 Total
23 Hard fats
24 Ones making snap decisions?
25 Passed quickly
27 Item of sports equipment approximately 43" long
28 The Sun Devils, for short
30 "Mr." whose first name is Quincy
31 Chili accompaniment, often
35 Slip
36 Bygone flier, for short
39 Street sign . . . or a hint to this puzzle's theme
40 ___-eyed
41 "Por ___ Cabeza" (tango song)
42 Incendiary
44 Like humans and ostriches
46 Former Ohio governor Strickland
47 One-eyed god of myth
51 Fruit waste
52 Paris's Rue ___ Croix de la Bretonnerie: Abbr.
54 ___-Roman
55 Cold and damp
57 Mountain climbing hazard
59 Doo-wop syllable
60 Batman, with "The"
62 Essential
63 Earthen pots for liquids
64 Big name in '50s TV
65 Fingers
66 Naughty
67 Scraps

DOWN

1 Point a finger at, say
2 Confine
3 Sartre novel, with "La"
4 Hastens
5 Quiet fishing spot
6 Company started in 1946 at the Detroit and Miami airports
7 Scratch
8 Red carpet walker
9 Shangri-las
10 Out the window
11 Like a saber
12 North Carolina county seat
13 Educ. group
18 Mad workers, for short
22 1992 top 10 hit "Life ___ Highway"
24 Companion of Panza
26 Knight time?
28 Tiger or Twin, briefly
29 Censors have them: Abbr.
30 E-mails: Abbr.
32 "Be ___!"
33 Last digit in a price, often
34 British author Bagnold
36 Benchwarmers
37 Sang
38 Features of many Olympic broadcasts
43 British fighter plane
45 G.P.'s grp.
48 More like a doornail?
49 Superlatively slippery
50 Frank who wrote "The Pit," 1903
52 Ingratiating behavior
53 Prepared, as a report
54 Dogfaces
56 Turn-of-the-century year in King John's reign
57 ___ chic
58 "That's enough out of you!"
59 What people who head for the hills do?
61 Popular TV drama set in Las Vegas

by David Chapus

ACROSS

1 Two drinks, for some
6 Reserved to a greater degree
11 1099-___ (tax form sent by a bank)
14 Japanese mushroom
15 Holmes of "Batman Begins"
16 Conjunction that usually has a partner
17 Eco-friendly in Las Vegas?
19 Rapping "Dr."
20 Tai chi instructor
21 Kind of account not used much anymore
23 Food glaze
25 Down Under springers
26 Omaha's waterfront during downpours?
32 Tax-free transaction, usually
33 Position on the Enterprise: Abbr.
34 Reception vessel
35 Cause ___
37 Actress Milano and namesakes
41 Charles I, II, III . . . or X
42 Had something
43 The Bobcats of the Mid-American Conference
44 First-place finishers in Bangor?
48 Planted
49 Feature of an essential oil
50 "Oh yes, I love that dress," maybe
53 Team in College Station, Tex.
58 ___ Thorpe, 2000 and 2004 Olympic swimming sensation
59 Jogging atop Great Falls?
61 Neatnik's opposite

62 Environs for Galatea, in myth
63 Banks in Chicago
64 Places with defibrillators, for short
65 Move along a buffet line, perhaps
66 They're found on staffs

DOWN

1 Stamina
2 Preceder of a case name
3 Plumbing fixture manufacturer
4 General store on "The Waltons"
5 Musician's weakness
6 Biathlon need
7 Milliners' securers
8 Home of Odysseus
9 ___, zwei, drei
10 Guns
11 Like fireworks, infrequently
12 "We can't squeeze any more in"
13 Some migrations
18 Woody vine with violet blossoms
22 Charles of "Death Wish"
24 Yearn (for)
26 Foreign policy advisory grp.
27 ___-necked
28 Shadow, so to speak
29 Having an effect
30 Ottoman sultan known as "the Magnificent"
31 Taste
36 Gift-wrapping aid
37 Part of Lawrence Welk's intro

38 "___ Hates Me," 2002 hit by Puddle of Mudd
39 Melody
40 Pad name
42 Kind of gland
44 High-luster fabric
45 "Dallas" kinfolk
46 Sprinkled
47 Unpleasant reminder?
48 Credit card action
51 Asteroid on which a NASA probe landed in 2001
52 ___ Baines Johnson (presidential daughter)
54 "Friday the 13th" staple
55 Places to sleep
56 Issue
57 Some Fr. honorees
60 Suffix with glass

by Laura Sternberg

ACROSS

1 What you might push a pushpin in
5 Dimwit, in Yiddish slang
10 International company with the slogan "Home away from home"
14 North African city captured by the Allies in 1942
15 In unison
16 1899 gold rush locale
17 A la ___ (nearby: Sp.)
18 David ___ George, British P.M., 1916–22
19 New growth
20 Start of a poem by Emily Dickinson that continues "But God be with the Clown, / Who ponders this tremendous scene"
23 Levels
24 Barker of the Cleveland Indians who pitched a perfect game in 1981
25 Increases
28 Refuge for David, in the Bible
32 Eur. monarchy
33 Poem, part 2
36 Christmas verse starter
38 Radio geek
39 Former Nebraska senator James
40 Poem, part 3
45 ". . . ___ he drove out of sight"
46 Chinese porcelain with a pale green glaze
47 Sleep disturbers
49 Sedona maker
50 Puts in a snug spot
52 Poem, part 4
58 Warren who founded a rental car company
59 Chew the scenery
60 Spray target
61 Pull-down list
62 Fix
63 It runs parallel to the radius
64 Teacher's before-class work
65 Volume unit
66 Overbrim (with)

DOWN

1 1977 best seller set at Boston Memorial Hospital
2 ___ contraceptive
3 Queen of Bollywood
4 Funnyman Don
5 Shipping mainstay of the 1600s
6 Physician William
7 Appears imminent
8 Singer with the 2008 gold record "And Winter Came . . ."
9 Acts the yenta
10 Double ___
11 The worst of times
12 "Lucky Jim" novelist, 1954
13 Relay division
21 South American monkey
22 ___ tide
25 Monkeyshine
26 Divine water
27 Say with two syllables where one would do, say
28 Promotional item
29 Philly hoopster
30 Extremely large, old-style
31 1985 Meg Tilly title role
34 In the past
35 Is afflicted by
37 Reorganizes drastically
41 Figure in the Edda
42 They have no ties
43 Rain forest implement
44 Sommer of Hollywood
48 Try to see
50 Antique dealer's happy discovery
51 Articulate
52 Anytime
53 Melon's site
54 Drop
55 Fallow
56 "___ But the Brave" (1965 Sinatra film)
57 Elderly relative, informally
58 Crank (up)

by Edward Safran

ACROSS

1 Yeshiva student
4 Happy sound
9 Crazy excited
14 The Cavaliers of the N.C.A.A.
15 Railroad between Illinois and Atlantic avenues
16 Bag
17 Co-creator of Dungeons & Dragons
19 N.B.A. star point guard Kidd
20 Award since 1956
21 Holiday servings
22 Sly
25 Is off guard
28 Fish whose skin is sometimes used for leather
29 Spread selection
30 French auto race
33 Its gatherings are smart things to attend
35 Beginner: Var.
36 N.L. team, on scoreboards
38 Squeeze (out)
39 Trademarked brand of waterproof fabric
42 Grp. with the 1979 hit "Don't Bring Me Down"
43 Rx specification
44 Indigo dye source
45 "Revolutionary Road" novelist Richard
47 Palate-raising response
51 Scourge
52 Sawbuck
53 Snake's bioweapon
54 Splitsville parties
55 Walk, e.g.
57 Raw material?
59 Weird Al Yankovic's "___ on Jeopardy"
61 Vaudeville brother born Milton

66 Starbucks size
67 Eddie Murphy's role in "Coming to America"
68 Fotos
69 BP competitor
70 Ex-lax?
71 Cuff

DOWN

1 Water holder
2 Actress Mendes
3 Drug ___
4 Old N.Y.C. club said to be the birthplace of punk
5 Harvesting for fodder
6 Ready to roll
7 Vitamin abbr.
8 Chicken ___
9 Financial daily, in brief
10 More ridiculous

11 Levy at a BP or 69-Across station
12 Part of an old Royal Navy ration
13 Urges
18 Dingbats
22 Streaker seen at night
23 Pub container
24 Thirtysomethings
26 Femur neighbor
27 Lather
28 Sticker?
31 "Forgot About ___" (2000 Grammy-winning rap song)
32 Compound used in aviation fuel
34 "F Troop" corporal
37 Michelangelo sculpture on a biblical subject
40 Billy Martin, for the Yankees

41 Musical phrase
46 Crosswise to a ship's keel
48 Irritates
49 Minstrel show figures
50 Annual event that includes motocross
55 Say "Uncle!"
56 "I'll take 'The New York Times Crossword Puzzle' for $200, ___"
58 It may need a big jacket
60 Word before ear or horn
61 Bit of "hardware"
62 Hi-strung instrument?
63 Police radio message: Abbr.
64 "Road to ___" (1947 flick)
65 Turkey, to a bowler

by Brendan Emmett Quigley

ACROSS

1 Garland native to Minnesota
5 Not in the buff
9 With 46-Down, site of Cape Breton Island
13 English artist John who's buried at St. Paul's Cathedral
14 Potential sucker
15 The brother in "Am I my brother's keeper?"
16 Lawyers: Abbr.
17 Nickname for a dwarfish piano prodigy?
19 Sleeping cave denizen?
21 "First Blood" hero John
22 Musical sound before and after "da"
23 Comic Dunn and others
24 Bank
27 Collected
30 Adaptable truck, for short
31 Pickled pub quiz winner?
36 Musical Mitchell
38 Said with a sneer
39 Icicle site
40 Ships carrying a smelly gas?
43 Domingo, for one
44 Deli machine
45 One begins "By the rivers of Babylon, there we sat down"
47 Toast
49 Parenthesis, essentially
50 It may be organized
51 Comfy kids?
57 Pride of 12?
59 Bring (out)

60 Part of ABM
61 Move like molasses
62 Combative retort
63 ___ Verde National Park
64 1974 Sutherland/Gould spoof
65 Contented sighs (and a homophonic hint to this puzzle's theme)

DOWN

1 Bruce Springsteen album "The Ghost of Tom ___"
2 ___ no good
3 Scatterbrain
4 Positive affirmation
5 Mobile home?
6 Counterpart of Apollo
7 Partially
8 Like 10-Down: Abbr.
9 Early Christian convert
10 Only president born in Hawaii
11 Shake, rattle and roll
12 High in the Sierra Madre?
17 "2001" studio
18 Maine university town
20 Unfeeling
23 Comparatively recent
24 1981 Stephen King novel
25 Complete
26 Ashcroft's predecessor
27 Like some waves
28 Online weekly, e.g.
29 Golf's ___ Cup
32 K. T. of country music
33 Early baby talk
34 Devilish

35 Chew (out)
37 People with this don't go out for very long
41 Actor Cary of "Twister"
42 Not at all stiff
46 See 9-Across
47 It can cure many things
48 Laugh-a-minute folks
49 Writer Rand
50 Chowder morsel
51 Prison, slangily
52 Black Sabbath singer, to fans
53 Pieces of pizza?
54 Celestial bear
55 Bite
56 Pontiacs of old
58 How many it takes to tango in Spain?

by Patrick Blindauer and Tony Orbach

ACROSS

1 Cry of anticipation
5 Low part
9 Synthetic fabric
14 Game with many balls
15 Carve
16 Cry of accomplishment
17 Revealed when seeking medical help?
20 1979 Fleetwood Mac hit
21 ___ Barry, with the 1965 hit "1-2-3"
22 Density symbol
23 "I've had it!"
26 Wing
27 Trixie's mom, in the comics
28 Santa ___
29 Instrument in the E Street Band
31 Focus of a hospital center
33 Water passages that don't turn?
37 Exhibitor of dorsiflexion
38 It's low for aces: Abbr.
39 Modern sales
42 One-named R&B singer makes her choice?
45 Locations of some secret meetings
47 Pink-slip
48 "Patience ___ virtue"
49 "___ you one!"
50 Drunk
52 Accomplished in
55 Old Vietnamese strongman ___ Dinh Diem
56 Slangy conjunction
57 A lot of a Maine forest
58 Continental salve?
64 ___ ceremony
65 Ending with flat or spy
66 Prefix with -plasm
67 Staffers: Abbr.
68 "___ View" (1999 Broadway play)
69 Flat, for short

DOWN

1 Approvals
2 Schemer's utterance
3 Sean ___ Lennon
4 Question that demands an explanation
5 Recuperation requirement
6 Boy lead-in
7 K.S.U., L.S.U. or M.S.U.
8 Bermuda memento, perhaps
9 Massachusetts town named for a river in England
10 Menace for Sinbad the sailor
11 HNO_2
12 God, in the Old Testament
13 Singer Julius who was famously fired on the air by Arthur Godfrey
18 Place for a headphone
19 American alternative
23 Zilch
24 "Come ___!"
25 "Just you wait!"
26 Derive (from) . . . or a two-part hint for understanding 17-, 33-, 42- and 58-Across
27 Drink that may be vanilla-flavored
30 "Just ___"
32 Cambodian currency
34 Advice for lovers whose parents disapprove
35 Copper
36 Tabula ___
40 "___ deal!"
41 Future atty.'s hurdle
43 Newsstand offering
44 They're under hoods
45 Hollywood business
46 Reprobates
51 Conductor noted for wearing white turtlenecks
53 "The Silmarillion" creature
54 Bone: Prefix
56 Inferiors to sgts.
57 Hurricane's force
59 ___ flakes
60 '60s service site
61 B and B
62 "Beauty is truth, truth beauty" genre
63 Approval

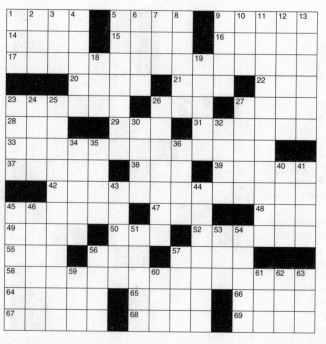

by Oliver Hill

ACROSS

1 Starring role
5 Way to go
9 Certain sultan's subject
14 "There was a time . . ."
15 It's headed by a deputy asst. secy. of labor
16 They need their bearings
17 See 71-Across
20 Romance fiction or horror films, e.g.
21 Midcentury year
22 European tongue
23 Small change
25 Letters at sea
27 See 71-Across
35 Basic education, familiarly
36 House support?
37 Language that contains no adjectives
38 Redolence
41 Do colorful work
43 Coffee break time, maybe
44 Generic
46 "I'll take that as __"
48 E.T.S. offering
49 See 71-Across
53 "Yes, __!"
54 Alternative to "roll the dice"
55 Band lineup
59 Microwave
61 Available
65 See 71-Across
68 Drill
69 Def Leppard hit "Pour Some Sugar __"
70 Approved
71 Shade that defines 17-, 27-, 49- and 65-Across

72 Title grp. in an ABC drama
73 Barbecue order

DOWN

1 High-priced ticket option
2 Great-great-great-grandfather of Methuselah
3 Electrical letters
4 Scrawl graffiti on, e.g.
5 Strength
6 Word with mountain or fly
7 Not us
8 Indigent
9 Klutz
10 Inspiration
11 Decor finish?
12 Us, abroad
13 Bikini, e.g.
18 Culminating point
19 Merlin of football and TV
24 Pointy-__
26 Rebounds, e.g.
27 Swiss capital
28 Documentarian Morris
29 Queen's attendant
30 Like some pyramids
31 "__ got you"
32 Having a bite
33 Almost 80 million people visit it yearly
34 Former Colorado governor Roy
39 Dallas hoopster, briefly
40 Where the Iowa Straw Poll is done
42 Goals
45 "My Fair Lady" lady

47 Fought against
50 One of Isabella I's kingdoms
51 "The Mod Squad" role
52 Mainstay
55 1970s–'80s singer Andy
56 Songwriter Novello
57 Urban sidewalk vendor's offering
58 Boatload
60 Pint-size
62 Golfer Isao __
63 Financial writer Marshall
64 Attorneys' degs.
66 Coastal flier
67 Great Brit., e.g., in years past

by Steve Dobis

ACROSS

1 Discombobulate
6 Reasons some games run long: Abbr.
9 You can get one on the house: Abbr.
13 Lines
15 *Final resting place for old autos?
17 Congo tributary
18 Cow or goat
19 Preceder of bravo in a radio alphabet
20 Showed joy, in a way
22 Canine command
23 Person on the left?: Abbr.
24 *Father of the Ziploc?
29 Extreme Atkins diet credo
32 "Ta-ta!"
33 Author Fallaci
35 Repel, with "off"
36 Pun-crimes committed by the answers to the six starred clues?
41 Like some primaries
42 Team esteem
43 Island attire
46 Like Gamal Abdel Nasser's movement
49 *Wide shoe specification?
51 Work, as a battle station
52 Wm. H. Taft was the only U.S. president born in this month
54 Show unease, maybe
56 ___-Pacific
57 Long key
61 Natural
63 *Recently opened sandwich shop?
64 It's white and fleecy
65 Parts of codes
66 Thataway
67 Crackers

DOWN

1 Pool shades
2 *Multiplyin' by 2?
3 Not heeding
4 ___ moth
5 REM researcher's tool
6 Food whose name comes from a language of West Africa
7 Big print maker
8 Interchangeable with, with "the"
9 Atlas abbr.
10 ___ degree
11 Rev
12 R.N.'s colleague
14 Home of the 2,700-mile-long Lena River
16 First secretary of homeland security
21 Mummify
23 It has feathers and flies
25 Original "Playboy"
26 Reddens, maybe
27 Tiptop
28 Bombs
30 Pinball machine, e.g.
31 Listen in (on)
34 Simple building
36 Outlay
37 On ___ with
38 Actress Gilpin of "Frasier"
39 Extremist
40 Personal flair
44 Like many checking accounts
45 With a silver tongue
47 Categorize
48 *Base of a fragrant tree?
50 Home of the Sawtooth Range
53 Violet variety
55 Sign of sheepishness
56 Start of a magic incantation
57 ___ Digital Short
58 Bit of a stew
59 "How cute!"
60 Bank offerings, in brief
62 Penpoint

by Greg Kaiser and Steven Ginzburg

49

ACROSS

1 B-ball player
6 Like the Grand Canyon or Fourth of July fireworks
15 "Casablanca" co-star
16 Phobic sort
17 Prayer leaders
18 Rush job?
19 Broadway Joe
21 "American Pie" actress Tara
22 "Burma Looks Ahead" author
23 Head of steam?
24 Give ___ (care)
26 Picasso's muse Dora ___
27 De ___ (by right)
29 Jocund
31 Cigar distributor, perhaps
36 Fictional hero on a quest to Mount Doom
40 Gets past a last difficulty . . . or a hint to this puzzle's theme
42 Creepy
43 Unisex
44 "Show pity, ___ die": "The Taming of the Shrew"
46 Heading in a Keats volume
47 "Notch" on Orion's belt
50 Diaper, in Devon
53 Mandela's org.
56 Agcy. with agents
57 Stuff the piggy bank
58 Take, as an exam
61 Means of some W.W. I raids
64 Complete, quickly
65 Ousters
66 Crunching sound
67 Welcome January 1, say
68 1950s fad item

DOWN

1 New York City tour provider
2 Bodies of organisms
3 Suspended air travel?
4 Humorist Bombeck
5 Kick back
6 Hill denizen
7 ___ smile (grin)
8 Calculus pioneer
9 Teeing off
10 Sud's opposite
11 Where you may get steamed
12 "The Taming of the Shrew" setting
13 1986 Turner autobiography
14 Showtime, at NASA
20 Strings pulled in heaven?
25 The end
26 Some aromatic resins
27 Sonny
28 Milk dispenser
30 Prior to, poetically
31 Paid intro?
32 Beluga delicacy
33 Joint possession word
34 ___ Beta Kappa
35 Classical storyteller
37 Series opener
38 Part of many Dutch surnames
39 Hosp. areas
41 Buffalo Bill ___ Wild West Show
45 Bad way to be caught
47 Teeny dress measurement
48 ___ Fountain
49 Clinton's first defense secretary
51 Par ___
52 Pasta variety
53 Run ___ of
54 Bellini opera
55 Mysterious art visible from the sky
57 Green of "The Italian Job," 2003
59 Scratcher's target
60 Dolly Parton's "Travelin' ___"
62 %: Abbr.
63 Milwaukee-to-Houston dir.

by Elizabeth C. Gorski

ACROSS

1 Shindigs
8 Elf costume add-ons, maybe
15 Overwhelmingly
16 Property receiver
17 Vitamin A
18 Game with four jokers
19 Qty.
20 Like loot, often
22 Caste member
23 Spilled the beans
25 Abbr. often repeated redundantly
26 Detection device
28 Monterrey month
30 Big truck
33 Big truck
34 Asian goatlike animal
35 Official gemstone of Alaska
36 ___ school
37 See 21-Down
40 Latin lesson word
43 "___ Gold," 1992 album that has sold 28 million copies worldwide
44 Preceded, with "to"
48 Apple, e.g.
49 Set
50 Loy of old Hollywood
51 Weak ones
53 Self-esteem
56 End of many company names
57 Cork's home: Abbr.
58 Unchanged
62 Boxer's handler?
63 Made safe
65 Composer Antonio
67 Sequestering, legally speaking
68 Cowardly
69 Trudge
70 Foreign currency unit

DOWN

1 1979 World Series champs
2 Literally, "daughter of the wind"
3 Mojave Desert sight
4 Prefix on many chemical compound names
5 + and – items
6 Make a big scene?
7 Comic book sound
8 A pop
9 Wings, zoologically
10 Orange coats
11 Leaves with a caddy?
12 More cracked
13 Sweets, e.g.
14 Cruise, say
21 What all the answers on this puzzle's 37-Across are to each other
24 Weight training unit
27 Fish-eating raptors
29 "You ___ me!"
31 Head light?
32 Pick up
35 Be in sync
38 Not the most authoritative journalism source
39 Slippery ___
40 "The one-l lama," to Ogden Nash
41 Funeral attendee
42 Result of butting heads?
45 Intended to convey
46 Upset
47 More sallow
52 Word with club or mine
54 Fill the tank
55 Rial spender
59 Layers
60 Sharpness
61 Island in the Arcipelago Toscano
64 Weapon first designed in 1950
66 Destination of many filings, for short

by David J. Kahn

ACROSS

1 1970 hit for the Jackson 5
4 "Deal!"
10 What a loose thread might be
14 Friendly term of address
15 Río crosser
16 Nest egg protectors
17 Name of Lord Rubble's feudal estate?
19 Slurs, in music
20 English princess
21 Sender of monthly checks: Abbr.
22 Fix, as a pump
24 Present addition
26 Air in a sooty shaft?
28 Removed roughly
32 Big Apple sch.
33 Sly little dog?
35 One stuck in the can
40 Third in a Latin series
41 Carefully search
43 Short evening?
44 Charles ___, "Brideshead Revisited" protagonist
46 Celebration for a Disney dwarf?
48 "The Mikado" wardrobe item
50 Like words?
51 Bamboozle a "Fargo" director?
56 Do sum work
57 Picasso/Braque movement
58 ___ Lingus
61 Title heroine described in the first sentence of her novel as "handsome, clever and rich"
64 It's shrinking in Asia
65 Property claim along the Rio Grande?
68 Realty ad abbr.

69 Alchemic knowledge
70 Mungojerrie or Skimbleshanks, in a musical
71 Wet septet
72 Toadies
73 P.G.A. Tour Rookie of the Year after Singh

DOWN

1 "Money, Money, Money" band
2 Muffin composition, maybe
3 Hot dog coating at a county fair
4 Mirror
5 "___ and Dolls"
6 Judges
7 Pioneer computer
8 Beach time in Bordeaux
9 Offset, as expenses
10 Gorge
11 Choisy-___ (Paris suburb)
12 Pawnbroker, in slang
13 Ruhr industrial hub
18 Recent arrival
23 Month before Tishri
25 Convex cooker
27 Betters
28 Romanov ruler
29 "___ Own" (song from "Les Miz")
30 DHL competitor
31 Sysop, for one
34 Place to overnight in an R.V.
36 Unbeliever
37 Meadow voles
38 Major conclusion?
39 Roger of "Cheers"
42 Sch. that's about 150 mi. north of 32-Across

45 Enormous birds of myth
47 Sumac from Peru
49 City visited in "Around the World in 80 Days"
51 Union foes
52 White-cap wearer
53 "The Audacity of Hope" author
54 Slumps
55 Pusher pursuers
59 Cheese choice
60 ___ Dubos, Pulitzer winner for "So Human an Animal"
62 Seder, e.g.
63 Creatures with tunnel vision?
66 Prospector's prize
67 Fled

by Patrick Blindauer

ACROSS

1 Not having big waves
5 Bandmaster from 1880 to 1931
10 The animals for Noah's Ark came in these
14 "Hard ___!" (captain's order)
15 Match
16 Stuck, after "in"
17 Something that's hard to close?
19 Relative of a hawk
20 Mirror
21 Editor's resource
23 Three times, in prescriptions
24 Nothing ___
26 George Knightley, to Emma Woodhouse
28 Prizes
30 Small amphibians
32 ___ Broad College of Business
33 What road hogs hog
34 City in Orange County, Calif.
35 Force felt on earth
36 Advice for the brokenhearted . . . or one of four arrangements found literally in this puzzle
39 Wedding rental
42 Like many a garden
43 Vintner Martini's associate
47 Mozart's "L'___ del Cairo"
48 It may start with "Starters"
49 Dweller on the Bay of Biscay
50 Fathers
52 Skin
54 Diggers' org.
55 Certain computer image format
57 Herbal beverage
59 Hungarian Communist leader ___ Kun
60 One in search of heretics
62 Go weak at the knees
63 Verges on
64 Split
65 Personal reserve funds, for short
66 Eliza Doolittle in "Pygmalion," e.g.
67 "___ Tú" (1974 hit)

DOWN

1 Financing
2 Tree-lined avenue
3 Houdini escape device
4 Where races are run
5 Browns
6 Giants of folklore
7 Ossuary, maybe
8 Samuel, e.g., in the Bible
9 Ford's first minivan
10 George of "Star Trek"
11 Set down
12 Shoe part that touches the floor
13 Marthe or Marie: Abbr.
18 "The Kingdom and the Power" author, 1969
22 Director Van Sant
25 Produce and present
27 Teamster's transport
29 ___ Park, N.Y.
31 Barn sackful
34 Blessing
35 Tribe met by Lewis and Clark
37 1960s Roger Moore TV series
38 Discount store offerings, for short
39 High pitch
40 Brew introduced in the 1990s
41 ___ Gorilla, 1960s cartoon title character
44 Sound before "That's all, folks!"
45 Gershwin's "___ to Watch Over Me"
46 Toward the center
48 '70s TV production co.
49 Cook, in a way, as beef
51 Les ___-Unis
53 "It's ___ bet!"
56 French tire
58 The Chieftains' home
59 Songwriters' grp.
61 African plant whose leaves are chewed as a stimulant

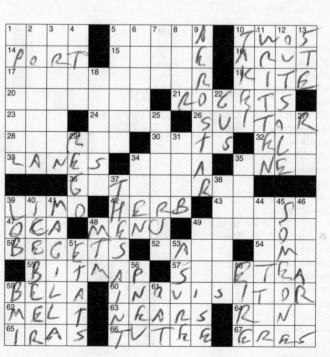

by Gary Cee

ACROSS

1 Source of the line "Frailty, thy name is woman!"
7 Some believers
13 Poor thing about a slouch
14 Vacation destinations
16 Dressed for a white-tie affair
17 Order in the court
18 Some urban digs
19 Shooter on the playground
21 Old Al Capp strip "___ an' Slats"
22 He preceded Joan at Woodstock
23 Former org. protecting depositors
25 Water collector
26 Mens ___ (criminal intent)
27 One who is no longer entitled
29 Golf club part
30 Set off, in a big way
32 Bigger-than-life persona
34 & 35 One who has done the circled things, combined, more often than any other major-league player
36 Attempts to strike
39 Georgia birthplace of Erskine Caldwell
43 Want ad abbr.
44 Cheese dish
46 Hotel addition?
47 U.S.N. brass: Abbr.
49 Photographic flash gas
50 Latin wings
51 Lab tube
53 Action stopper
54 "Can ___ Witness" (Marvin Gaye hit)
55 ___ Sánchez, co-director of "The Blair Witch Project"

57 Turned a blind eye toward
59 Last of the French?
60 Lemonlike fruit
61 Spoke rudely to
62 Classic brand of liniment

DOWN

1 Mother, on the second Sunday in May
2 Whence Elaine, in Arthurian lore
3 Highest peak in the Philippines: Abbr.
4 Baseball All-Star Tiant
5 Goethe's "The ___-King"
6 Where to take an exam
7 Attract
8 Fish that may be caught in a cage
9 Puerto Rico, por ejemplo
10 Gathers on a surface, chemically
11 Reason for a medley, perhaps
12 Apostle called "the Zealot"
13 Enterprise-D captain
15 Permeated, with "into"
20 On the safe side
23 Political proposal from some conservatives
24 Fill, as with a crayon
27 Lend ___
28 Kind of button
31 Special ___
33 Breast enlargement material

35 Branch of technology
36 Like some spoonfuls
37 Salt add-ins
38 Japanese restaurant offering
39 Restaurant offering
40 Bank controller
41 Tidies
42 Rastafarian's do, for short
45 34 & 35-Across's 4,256 career hits, e.g.
48 Penn and others
50 Pythagoras' square
52 Speaker of the diamond
54 Digging
56 Near failure
58 Apt name for an ichthyologist?

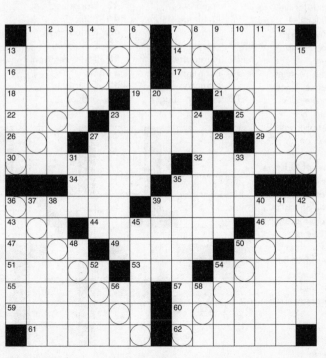

by Peter A. Collins and Joe Krozel

54

Note: After finishing this puzzle, color the circled squares blue, and color all the Across answers containing an "R" red, to reveal an image related to the puzzle's theme.

ACROSS

1 Bikini blast
6 Car wash aid
9 Bugs
13 Track branch
17 Film character played by a full-blooded Cherokee
18 Ear: Prefix
19 Cry
20 Name, in a way
21 Ferrari competitor
22 Dorm V.I.P.'s
23 Suburb south of Paris
24 Give a star, say
25 Japanese dog
26 Trendy prefix
27 Cultural org.
28 iPod contents
29 Spruce
30 "Heads for the hills" locale?
33 It may be fired
34 Poker champ Ungar
35 Actress Mendes
36 Whence "Thine alabaster cities gleam" lyric
46 Baseballer with a "W" on his cap
47 Kilmer of "Batman Forever"
48 Mideast capital
49 1775 flag motto
56 Actress Moran and others
57 Stock
58 Lucy of "Kill Bill"
59 Drunk's woe, with "the"
60 Bikers may have them
61 Some RCA products
62 Take on
63 Knack

64 ___ area
65 The right point?
66 Kind of salad
67 "Holy smokes!"
68 Pupil, in Picardie
69 Three-point shot, in slang
70 ". . . ___ he said"
71 Chariot attachment?
72 Pony farm sign

DOWN

1 Hawk's home
2 Lined up the cross hairs
3 Name
4 Possible result of anxiety
5 ". . . ___ the least"
6 "Air Music" composer
7 Not free
8 Turn bad
9 "Forget it!"
10 Pinker, perhaps
11 Hawaiian tourist attraction
12 Hugger-mugger

13 Rugby scuffle
14 Softly
15 Total
16 "The Terminator" man Kyle ___
28 "___ so?!"
31 ___ León (Mexican state bordering Texas)
32 "Law & Order" spinoff, informally
37 U.N.-like
38 Wheels
39 Oil production site?
40 Operator's need
41 Stately thing in Browning's "Oh, to be in England . . ."
42 Like Bar-Ilan University
43 Blacked out
44 Rattle
45 Rodeo rings?
49 Bed cover
50 Jazz's Peterson
51 Sip
52 Delectable
53 Buenos ___

54 As a result of
55 Aromatic compound
56 Whom Bugs bugs
62 "The Wire" shower

by Alex Boisvert

ACROSS

1 Examines a passage
6 Low islands
10 Some Morgan Stanley announcements, for short
14 Maker of Gauntlet and Area 51
15 Cousin of a heckelphone
16 Oscar winner Sorvino
17 Hospital employee's role as an opera girl?
19 Lord, e.g.
20 Swear words?
21 Mattress brand
22 Tiramisu topper
23 Locales for some orators
25 Attorney general before Reno
26 What Starkist decided to do for "Charlie"?
31 Circles overhead?
34 Carbonium and others
35 Boom preceder
36 Grace period?
37 Hard-to-refute evidence in court
39 Boarding zones: Abbr.
40 Veto
41 Does some floor work
42 In turmoil
43 A girl, born 8:48 a.m., weighing 6 pounds 13 ounces, e.g.?
47 You might be safe with them
48 Came out
52 Trajectories
54 Where some dye for a living
56 Band from Japan
57 Hollow response
58 Where a Hungarian toy inventor vacations in the Caribbean?
60 McAn of footwear
61 Valuable deposits
62 Goof-off
63 Orphan of literature
64 1976 top 10 hit for Kiss
65 Talk radio's G. Gordon ___

DOWN

1 Indian royalty
2 Exercise performed on a bench
3 Singer Neville
4 Vets, e.g.: Abbr.
5 Shop-closing occasions
6 Not cultured
7 Slightly
8 His planet of exile is Dagobah
9 Last word of "America the Beautiful"
10 BMW, e.g.
11 Cobbler bottoms
12 Three-layer snack
13 Title sister played by Shirley MacLaine, 1970
18 ". . . bad as they ___"
22 Burmese and others
24 Not long from now
25 Most of the Ten Commandments, basically
27 A little stiff?
28 Furrow maker
29 Almost perfect?
30 Number two: Abbr.
31 Full house, e.g.
32 Gérard's girlfriend
33 Villain from DC
37 Pirouette points
38 Shower time: Abbr.
39 Train in a ring
41 Court stars, maybe, in brief
42 Knife, e.g.
44 Returnee's "hello!"
45 "Yum!"
46 Every which way
49 Creator of "Dick Tracy"
50 Fell back
51 Holder of secrets, often
52 Black ___, archnemesis of Mickey Mouse
53 Sore
54 "You betcha!"
55 Support when one shouldn't
58 Take the wrong way?
59 Year Saint Innocent I became pope

by Patrick Blindauer

ACROSS

1 Formal club: Abbr.
6 Places to press the flesh?
10 Spirited cries
13 Some arts and crafts
16 Red remover, maybe
17 Bonuses
18 It's just a formality
19 "Follow me"
21 Motel extra
22 Diminutive endings
24 Apple pie companion?
25 States
27 Sp. title
29 Psychos
31 Leave in the dust, say
33 Long introduction?
34 English town near Windsor Bridge
37 General on a Chinese menu
38 Hinged pair of pictures
41 ___-Foy, Que.
42 Kind of blocker
44 Start of a Chinese game
45 Either of two emcees
47 Where "wikiwiki" means "to hurry"
49 "The Shelters of Stone" author
50 Clip
52 Anchorage-to-Fairbanks dir.
54 Signs on for another tour
57 Result of an emergency call, maybe
58 Get too big for
61 Prefix with -logy
62 Philemon, e.g.
64 Like the Trojan horse
66 Oil source
67 Starting instruction
68 What circles lack
69 Garden hose problems

DOWN

1 Craggy crest
2 "Tell me!"
3 ← Plastered
4 JFK : New York :: ___ : Chicago
5 ← Gambling game
6 RR building
7 ← Sherlock Holmes novel, with "The"
8 Heat
9 Methods: Abbr.
11 Part of a sob
12 Rarely read letters
13 Race before a race
14 20-vol. work
15 Wee hour
20 ← One starting a career, perhaps
23 Drop the ball
26 Migration formation?
28 Inner self
30 Record label of Bill Haley and His Comets
31 Gambling site: Abbr.
32 Milk
35 What buzzer beaters may lead to, briefly
36 What you keep
39 ___ Desert
40 ← Work period
43 Like some baseball teams
46 Tee follower
48 Penned
50 Archaeological find
51 Cabbie's line
53 Parts of a joule
55 Call that may result in an abrupt hang-up
56 Math figures
59 Diminutive ending
60 Crumb
63 Snake's warning
65 Cost-of-living meas.

by Bill Zais

ACROSS

1 Not stay fully upright
5 Flower in Chinese embroidery
10 Year the Chinese poet Li Po was born
14 People conquered by the Spanish
15 Fuse
16 10 to 1, e.g.
17 Cabinet dept.
18 Tangy teatime treats
20 Pittsburgh-born poet who was the subject of a Picasso portrait
22 Like some coincidences
23 Virgil hero
26 Surveillance device
28 Denture maker's need
30 Raw materials for shipbuilding
31 Spoil
33 Payola, e.g.
34 Famous quote by 20-Across
38 Spinners?
39 Who wrote "Can one be a saint if God does not exist?"
40 Let fly
41 "Spring ahead" hrs.
42 Baked comfort food
47 "Likewise"
49 "___ will ever guess!"
50 Colorful decoration hinted at by 34-Across
55 Carrie Bradshaw had one in "Sex and the City"
57 Kind of poker
58 Mine, to Manet
59 "___ X" (2003 Lisa Kudrow film)

60 Province of Saudi Arabia
61 German cathedral city
62 That is
63 "America" pronoun

DOWN

1 Subjects studied by medieval scholars?
2 Seriously committed
3 Rush
4 Part of a war plan
5 Berg opera
6 Linear
7 It may be on your side
8 They're involved in some reported abductions
9 Twisted this clue's is
10 Sink accessories
11 Wife of Julius Caesar
12 Rib or short loin
13 "___ alive!"
19 Informal top
21 Subject of the 1999 best seller "Dutch"
24 Writer Bierce
25 157.5 degrees from N
27 Gloomy
28 Attended
29 Smith of note
32 Inexpensive pens
33 Buffalo's Triple-A baseball team
34 Snow White's sister
35 "Don't play me for a dummy"
36 Get comfy
37 Was revolting
38 Wave function symbol in physics
41 Cabbage
43 Tails partner

44 Like Chopin
45 Embarrassing way to be caught
46 Character in "Piglet's Big Movie," 2003
48 Response to a stomach punch
51 Slightly
52 Money replaced by the euro
53 Mil. awards
54 "___ the jackpot!"
55 Bag, in brand names
56 Med. group

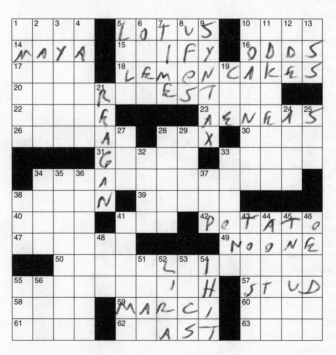

by Elizabeth C. Gorski

ACROSS

1 Taps may be heard in them
6 Debra of "The Ten Commandments"
11 Joe Friday's employer, for short
15 "See you later, alligator"
16 National alternative
17 Bogotá bears
18 [I don't care]
19 TROT?
21 HATER?
23 Bursts of energy?
24 Gut reaction?
25 Westerns
27 Teensy
28 ___ Harbour, Fla.
29 N.F.L. position: Abbr.
31 "Rough winds do shake the darling buds of ___": Shak.
32 Love all, say
34 Broadcasting
36 RIFTS?
39 San Juan native, slangily
40 Cold shower?
41 Sioux Falls-to-St. Paul dir.
42 1040 ID
43 Tattoo, in slang
44 Mother, in British dialect
47 Z producer
50 Tallahassee sch.
51 Tent event
52 GATES?
56 HOSE?
57 Walks
58 World's largest particle physics lab
59 Two-time Banderas role
60 Stern, for one
61 Beliefs
62 Some blades
63 Attempt some Internet fraud

DOWN

1 Snack item whose name suggests a 42-Down?
2 Stick
3 Las Vegas attraction, with "The"
4 Serves, say
5 Army NCO
6 Cruisers
7 "Half ___ is better . . ."
8 First senator in space
9 CPR experts
10 Lethargy
11 Lite
12 In unison
13 Many a White House artwork
14 Mil. honor
20 She, in Brasilia
22 Clink preceder
26 Neighbor of Turk.
28 Cap'n's underling
29 Street ___
30 Racket makers?
32 Colt fans, for short?
33 Augury
34 Stop on the Trans-Siberian Railway
35 Originally
36 Paint and shellac, for example
37 Power outage cause
38 Coffee mate?
39 Rapper MC ___
42 Cold response?
44 Drink at Trader Vic's
45 Hello and goodbye
46 Good guy
48 Composer Camille Saint-___
49 U.S.D.A. part: Abbr.
50 Renaissance ___
51 Store that's hard to find
53 Each
54 Truth alternative
55 "You're ___, ya know that?": Archie Bunker
56 58-Across subj.

by Ashish Vengsarkar

ACROSS

1 Recreating
7 Commercial prefix with vision
10 Election night figs.
14 Ships whose rudders don't touch water
16 Sounds heard in a bowl
17 35-Across of 57-Across that equals 12-Down
18 Medical suffix
19 Bobsled challenges
20 Aesthete
22 The Big East's Panthers, for short
23 They travel through tubes
24 Winter driving hazards
26 Start of a Hemingway title
28 Less affluent
29 French novelist Robert ___, upon whose work the 1973 thriller "The Day of the Dolphin" is based
31 Philosopher Zeno of ___
32 Signature piece?
35 See 17- and 57-Across
38 Nav. rank
39 Container for folding scissors
41 Something a chair may hold
42 Pie crust pattern
45 Rubber gaskets
49 Endocrinological prefix
50 Status follower
51 Tolkien villains
53 Destination of Saul when he had his conversion, in the Bible

55 Reader of someone else's diary, say
56 Sparkling wine source
57 35-Across of 17-Across that equals 12-Down
59 Mideast's Gulf of ___
60 Neither high nor low
61 Half-dome construction
62 Govt. ID
63 First arrival

DOWN

1 "Take ___ breath"
2 Swiss cheese
3 Cry just before a rabbit appears?
4 Dwells in the past?
5 So, so long
6 Feminine side

7 Extraordinary
8 Red-spotted ___
9 Singer of the Wagner aria "Liebestod"
10 Be a breadwinner
11 Detective's work record
12 Either 17- or 57-Across
13 Snake's warning
15 3.3 in a transcript, maybe
21 Lead from a mountain?
23 Brickmaking need
25 Women of Andalucía: Abbr.
27 Drs.' org.
28 With clammy hands, say
30 N.Y.C. airport

32 Gymnastics coach Károlyi
33 Possible title for this puzzle
34 Deep discounts
36 Britain's Royal ___ Club, for plane enthusiasts
37 1051, on a monument
40 Complete the I.R.S.'s Schedule A
43 ___ fog
44 Bob at the Olympics
46 Puzzled
47 Dig, with "on"
48 Servings at teas
50 Doyenne
52 Like L-O-N-D-O-N
54 100-lb. units
55 Bear's warning
56 Simile center
58 Flashed sign

by Elizabeth C. Gorski

ACROSS

1 Show-off
4 Manx cries
9 U.S. Marine
14 "Wheel of Fortune" purchase
15 Leader of the pack
16 Like some flocks
17 Neurotic cartoon character
18 End of the line, e.g.
19 Auto debut of 1989
20 Bullet train type
22 Go for
24 Hosp. locations
25 Innards
27 Common sports injury site
28 Certain occupation
31 Milo's canine pal
32 See 4-Down
33 "Star Trek" empath
34 Animal control officer
36 Folded corner
37 Trail
38 1927–31 Ford
42 Alexander ___, Russian who popularized a chess opening
44 Hibernia
46 G.I.'s ID
47 Person who raises and sells pups
49 City containing a country
50 Big rig
53 "Get ___!"
54 Plotted for urban uses
55 Cans
56 Entertains
58 "Holy moly!"
59 20 places?
60 Cry that may accompany pounding
64 Using base 8
66 Steal
68 ___ Miss
69 One bit
70 One falling into good fortune
71 NBC-TV inits.
72 Old sailor
73 Animal in a lodge
74 Cutthroat

DOWN

1 Damage
2 Ready to serve
3 Kraft Foods drink
4 With "the" and 32-Across, describing an old Matryoshka doll
5 Hgts.
6 Antonym: Abbr.
7 Hit song from 2000 . . . and a hint to 10 symmetrically arranged Across answers
8 Mocking, in a way
9 Loser to Clinton
10 The 31st vis-à-vis the 1st, e.g.
11 She-foxes
12 Habituates
13 Inferior
21 Super Bowl of 2023
23 K2 locale
26 Mac, e.g.
27 Many a Kirkuk resident
28 Dance bit
29 "Dies ___"
30 Injury, in law
34 Lascaux paintings, e.g.
35 Long, long time
37 With 48-Down, for example, south of the border
39 Cornwallis's school
40 Pricey fabric
41 Yellowing, maybe
43 Parts of box scores: Abbr.
45 Sitcom with the character B.J.
48 See 37-Down
49 Shot up
50 Some Girl Scout cookies
51 First-and-second bet
52 A little nuts
54 Feature of a pleasant summer day
57 "Two Treatises of Government" writer
59 Friend
61 It has two holes
62 Arms runner?
63 Stone, e.g.
65 PC key
67 Not delay

by Gary and Stephen Kennedy

61

ACROSS

1 Facility
5 ← What this is, on a calendar
8 Signals
12 Jiltee of myth
14 Yamaha offering, in brief
15 Perform acceptably
16 Profanities (and a hint to this puzzle's anomalies)
19 Peer group?
20 Razz
21 Liverpool-to-Portsmouth dir.
23 Buzzers
25 Some exchanges, quickly
28 Arrives
30 Mean mien
32 Scale range
33 Do what Jell-O does
34 Alley of Moo
35 Patient responses
36 Geisha's accessory
37 Like
38 Many "Star Wars" fighters
40 Blood, e.g.
42 Forward
43 Some people in a tree
44 Division of an office bldg.
45 Wasn't straight
46 Carry-___
47 Garden sights
49 Is behind
51 Record holders? (and a punny hint to this puzzle's anomalies)
58 Sluggish
59 Whistle blower
60 Former "American Idol" judge
61 "Man oh man!"
62 ___ admin (computer techie)
63 Hip

DOWN

1 Voltaic cell meas.
2 Abbr. in a help-wanted ad
3 E-mail address ending
4 Like H. P. Lovecraft among all popular writers?
5 Show types
6 Part of a 2005 SBC merger
7 Actress Mimieux of "Where the Boys Are"
8 Offering, as a price
9 12 or 15 min.
10 Rx abbr.
11 Peck parts: Abbr.
13 Iranian supreme leader ___ Khamenei
15 100 lbs.
17 Some musical notes
18 Football linemen: Abbr.
21 They may have niños and niñas
22 Exit
24 Royal son of the comics
26 Nuclear unit
27 Merchants
28 Stuff on a shelf
29 Kowtower
30 Squeals
31 Cans
33 Courtroom identification
36 Starts of some sporting events
39 Big chip off the old block?
40 Health supplement chain
41 Defended
43 Pergolas
45 Dance grp. at the Met
48 It goes over a plate
50 ___ leash
51 Horse and buggy
52 Official lang. of Barbados
53 Part of a violin
54 Hardly macho
55 Actress Williams of the 1960s–'70s
56 ___ Lopez (chess opening)
57 On the ___

by Ashish Vengsarkar

ACROSS

1 Commercial name that literally means "to the skies"
5 Shouts while shaking pompoms
9 Break
13 "___ 18" (Leon Uris novel)
14 "Law & Order: S.V.U." actor
15 Insurance figure
16 Opposite of hinder
17 *Privilege
19 *No matter
21 Milch : German :: ___ : Italian
22 Common seal
25 Virgil described its "roar of frightful ruin"
28 New Deal org.
29 Use the answer to any of this puzzle's starred clues in ordinary conversation?
31 *And so forth
35 Lady of the Haus
36 *Ways things are said
40 All ___
41 *Sign to look elsewhere
42 Check out
43 Comedian Margaret
46 Some fund-raisers
47 One side in Mideast talks
50 Peak for Zeus, in Homer
54 *Stumbled upon
57 *As it's widely believed
60 Morales of "NYPD Blue"
61 Stocking caps, e.g.
62 Rock's Mötley ___
63 24-Down replacement
64 Ammonium particles, e.g.
65 Gets ready, with "up"
66 Rick with the 1976 #1 hit "Disco Duck"

DOWN

1 Modern letters
2 Scales seen at night
3 Ready
4 Age range for most first-year college students
5 TV host Kelly
6 One-hit wonder?
7 Range rovers
8 Hot
9 Much, slangily
10 News inits.
11 John
12 Cause of some skin burns
15 Conspirator against Caesar
18 Backpack fill
20 Really irk
23 "Vive ___!"
24 Coin with a laurel branch on the back
26 Modern: Ger.
27 Son of Prince Valiant
30 Kennedy's secretary of state
31 Individual and team event at the Olympics
32 Imaging lab output
33 Actor Feldman
34 Here, to Javier
35 Tournament favorite
37 Suffix with sex
38 Had
39 Juan's words of affection
43 Informal byes
44 Unlikely Oscar nominees
45 Without a break
48 Sales slips: Abbr.
49 New York hockey player
51 Put out
52 "The Wreck of the Mary ___"
53 Informal bye
55 Object under a magnifying glass, maybe
56 Some whiskeys
57 Make tracks?
58 Formula ___ (Italian auto racing)
59 A.T.M. need

by Dan Naddor

ACROSS

1 "A peculiar sort of a gal," in song
4 Muddy
8 Themed events
13 Actor Tognazzi of "La Cage aux Folles"
14 Seaside raptor
15 Allen Iverson's teammates till '06
16 Ingredient in some gum
18 Gossip
19 Request that often follows "Please"
20 Inceptions
21 Chow
22 Oscar Wilde or Bill Maher, for example
25 Some car roofs
27 Like some announcements that have been lost
28 Sister who's won the U.S. Open four times
30 Grafton's "___ for Innocent"
31 Curly shape
32 Starts of some games . . . and of the answers to 16-, 22-, 48- and 56-Across?
36 R.B.I. producer, sometimes: Abbr.
39 Holder of le trône
40 Minnesota college
44 "Hold on!"
47 Hot, after "on"
48 Like some passes
51 Mambo king Puente
52 Contravenes
53 They give you control
55 Fang
56 Cedar and hemlock
57 Lightly sprayed
58 Mathematician Post or Artin
59 Riddle-me-___
60 Foreign thoughts
61 Kind of column
62 New Left org.

DOWN

1 Hackneyed movie endings
2 Perturb
3 G.P.S. device, e.g.
4 Part of AARP: Abbr.
5 Small African antelope
6 "Back ___" (1974 Genesis song)
7 Family name of about 15% of Koreans
8 Big bomb
9 Runs out
10 Having a dividing wall, in biology
11 Locks
12 Map abbr. until 1991
15 TV Guide info
17 How many writers work
20 Buck ___, first black coach in Major League Baseball (Cubs, 1962)
23 Opening
24 Patriot's concerns, briefly
26 ___-Cat
29 What machmeters measure
33 Songs from rosy-cheeked singers, maybe
34 Moms and dads belong to it: Abbr.
35 Rather
36 Bad record, for short
37 Not a long-term solution
38 Certain plate
41 Overstays?
42 Not the same anymore
43 Gets ready to brush, maybe
45 This evening, on posters
46 Organic compounds with nitrogen
49 Step heavily (on)
50 Start of a counting rhyme
54 Like Clark Kent's manner
55 Third year in the reign of Edward the Elder
56 Corp. honcho

by Patrick McIntyre

64

ACROSS

1 Big name in oil
7 Easter flower, in Is-sur-Tille
10 Butterfly wings, e.g.
14 The fool in "A fool and his money are soon parted"
16 Tabula ___
17 Excuse given for asking for a ride
18 Humanoid trees in Tolkien
19 Ticks, say: Abbr.
20 Toddler's attire
21 Time for potty training, maybe
22 Rests
25 Chorus line opener
27 Handel cantata "___ e Leandro"
28 Promgoers, e.g.: Abbr.
29 Burning
32 Not shaky
34 Jagged
35 Clinks overseas
36 What's revealed by connecting the special squares in this puzzle in order
39 Start of the United Negro College Fund slogan
40 Kosher
41 ___ Szewinska, Olympic sprinting gold medalist of 1964, 1968 and 1976
42 Want from
43 Ab ___ (from the top)
46 Partisan leader?
47 Tube top
49 Daze
51 Nice kind of workweek
53 G.M., Ford and Chrysler
56 Setting for an Agatha Christie novel
57 Proctor's call
58 Advice for essay writers
61 Dickens creep
62 Eight producers?
63 Payroll dept. figs.
64 Wiring experts: Abbr.
65 Paris palace

DOWN

1 Middles that are often too big
2 Ingratiate
3 Has on hand
4 Intuit
5 When Canada celebrates Thanksgiving: Abbr.
6 Washington in the Songwriters Hall of Fame
7 Hawaiian strings?
8 You might get one before a party
9 Direct
10 Neck of the woods
11 Tony-winning "Frost/ Nixon" actor
12 Constellation
13 Best Director of 1992 and 2004
15 Be an utter bore?
23 Beer from upstate New York
24 Like the symmetry of a starfish
26 Free of charge
30 Part of some chains: Abbr.
31 Walks unsteadily
33 ___ cloud (region of comets far beyond Pluto)
34 Celtic land
35 "Beauty and the Beat" band
36 P.D.Q. Bach's "Sanka Cantata" and such
37 Final words of Numbers 5:22
38 Albanian coin
41 How mini-pizzas are usually cut
42 Each
43 Sounds off
44 1958 #1 song with the lyric "Let's fly way up to the clouds"
45 Bully's warning
48 Old comic strip "___ an' Slats"
50 Concord
52 O.K.'s from the O.K. Corral?
54 Exits
55 School basics
59 Presidential nickname
60 Square dance partner

by Elizabeth C. Gorski

ACROSS

1 Moccasin adornment
5 Faux pas
9 Took ___ (went swimming)
13 & 14 Nancy Lopez and Annika Sorenstam have each won this several times
16 Russo who co-starred in "The Thomas Crown Affair"
17 Literary lead role for Gregory Peck in 1956
18 Run ___ of
19 Clinched
20 Alphabet trio
21 Keyboard key
22 Boot feature
24 Singer Corinne Bailey ___
25 Bring into being
27 Intros
29 New York's ___ Institute (art school)
32 Straying
33 Brother-and-sister dancing duo
36 Out on the water
37 C₇H₅N₃O₆
38 Foolish chatter
41 Educ. course in which grammar and idioms are taught
42 Verified, in a way
44 Most merciless
46 Stereo component
49 Those against
50 Joins
52 *First row*
56 Online gasp
57 "You're the ___" (Cole Porter classic)
58 Popular ISP
59 Brazilian hot spot
60 ___ Beach, Fla.
62 Muscle connector
64 *Fourth row*
65 Paradise lost
66 Have a hankering
67 Suffix akin to -trix
68 Comedic star Martha
69 Many August babies
70 Guinea pigs, maybe

DOWN

1 Mont ___
2 Ancient Spartan magistrate
3 Wide open
4 *Fifth row*
5 Result of poor ventilation
6 Boost
7 Japanese butler in "Auntie Mame"
8 Mickey Mouse's puppy pal
9 Shipping magnate Onassis
10 Shrinks
11 Passionately
12 Support for the arts?
15 Act without the parents' blessings, say
21 "Don't go in there! It's ___!"
23 Always, poetically
26 Fitting
28 Lobby in a D.C. building?
30 ___ ll razor
31 Neon ___
33 Gene Roddenberry-inspired sci-fi series
34 Metallic shade, in Sheffield
35 Knock out
37 Upsets
39 Disappointments
40 Architect Saarinen
43 *Third or sixth row*
45 Suffix akin to -trix
47 Intersected
48 Like plain text
51 *Second row*
53 Classic Broadway musical with the song "Alice Blue Gown"
54 Bigger than big
55 Intersecting points
58 Aviation-related
61 *Seventh row*
63 Edinburgh refusal
64 Up on things, daddy-o

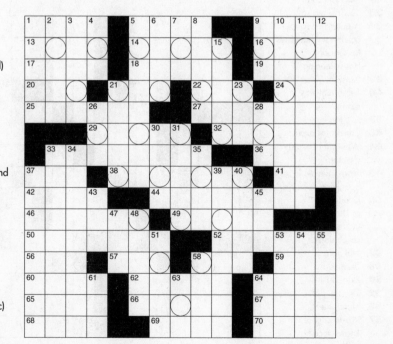

by Derek Bowman

ACROSS

1 English poet Coventry ___, who wrote "The Angel in the House"
8 Where "Thy will be done," in a prayer
15 Parts of irises
16 Cheap cafe
17 Scheme
18 Like outcasts
19 Balkan land
20 Canadian prov. on Atlantic Time
21 Previously called
22 Desert water source
24 Big 12 sch.
26 Bleed (for)
29 It can turn up heads
30 Rifle part
33 Skate part
34 Profitability, for a business
35 Not just a brat
36 "___ always say . . ."
37 Popular newspaper columnist who writes for Good Housekeeping
39 Sense of "wow"
40 Tricky highway maneuvers
42 ___ fault
43 Checks for accuracy
44 Where a hole may develop
45 Town in W.W. II headlines
46 Counterpart of Thanatos, in Freudian psychology
47 Not here
48 Stashes
50 Plant bristle
52 Tiny bit
53 Not authentic
57 World capital known locally as Krung Thep Mahanakhon

60 Overused soap opera plot device
61 Not to the point, say
62 Swordplay, e.g.
63 Runs down
64 Sack and others

DOWN

1 Have heat
2 Ending with buck
3 ___ place
4 Item on a chain
5 Twin Tony whose #6 jersey was retired
6 *Auto accessory
7 Sioux Falls-to-Cedar Rapids dir.
8 Dwell
9 Soft drink since 1924
10 Liquide clair
11 ___ Taylor (clothier)
12 *Crewman on the tail of a bomber
13 Corner
14 Fictional Mr.
20 *"Cheers!" . . . or a hint to answering this puzzle's five starred clues
23 Sweat
24 "Aha!"
25 "My dear fellow"
26 One in an affair
27 Holder of a black marker
28 *1968 Barbra Streisand starring role
31 Purchase by Mr. Fix-It
32 Lock
35 *Beef cut
37 Chopped

38 Kansas town on the Neosho River
41 Fake blood, maybe
43 Skiffs and scows
45 Fountain orders
49 Beneficiary
50 Opposite of up
51 You might catch one near a beach
52 Chocolate brand
54 Goddess who restored Osiris to life
55 Highest score in baccarat
56 Comedian's stock
58 Fed. purchasing org.
59 Kipling novel
60 Hyperactivity may be a sign of it, for short

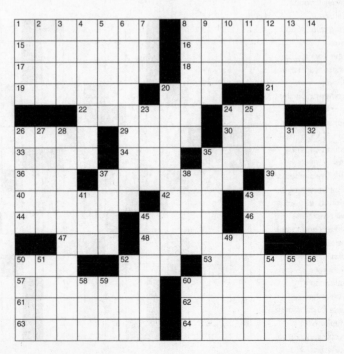

by C. W. Stewart

ACROSS

1 "Quién ___?" (Spanish "Who knows?")
5 Player on the 1979 N.B.A. championship team, for short
10 "Where's ___?"
14 Prefix with port
15 TV news host ___ Regan
16 Zero ___
17 First: Abbr.
18 "Mona Lisa," e.g.
20 Football formation
22 Literary inits.
23 Individual retirement account, e.g.
24 "___ salute!" (Italian drinking toast)
25 Must, with "to"
28 Scottish refusal
29 Somewhat overdone
31 Bush solicitor general Theodore
34 Shoe part
35 Lago composition
36 TV's Houston and Dillon
37 ___-turn
38 Geographical finger
39 Fictional governess
40 On ___ track
41 Parks and others
42 Pain
44 Vert.'s opposite
45 Place to get a 47-Across
46 Ball catcher
47 Work for a certain therapist
51 Some sweepers sweep them: Abbr.
52 Bartender's announcement
53 Voice of Scar in "The Lion King"
57 Asia's ___ Sea
58 Big-screen beekeeper
59 Stand for something?
60 Actress Anderson
61 Last name in mystery
62 Chip ___, whom many consider the greatest cash game poker player of all time
63 Remnants

DOWN

1 Aired
2 Raptor's roost
3 Cloud nine
4 Composition of a 30-Down
5 Pie-in-the-face giver or receiver
6 Circular seal
7 Memphis's locale
8 AOL, e.g.
9 Bravo follower
10 First number in a record
11 Not pro
12 Chaney of horror
13 Half a ring
19 ___ ease
21 Pintos, e.g.
24 Smirnoff competitor
25 Sci-fi awards
26 Honda division
27 Herringlike catch
29 Narrowly, after "by"
30 Theme of this puzzle
31 They can be read by the illiterate
32 Easy shot
33 Small groove
34 Actually
38 Nixon interviewer
40 More nervous
43 Friendliness
44 Pain
47 They're located behind the ears
48 Claire's boy on "Lost"
49 Sweat ___
50 ___ Island
51 Portly pirate
52 Get checkmated
53 Olympic sport since 1964
54 Old bridge expert Culbertson
55 Rod's partner
56 Actress Charlotte

by Kevan Choset

68

ACROSS

1 Finishes, with "up"
5 Like most radios
9 Jordan's only seaport
14 #13 in the Bronx, informally
15 Fair distance
16 Daybreak
17 Stage arches
19 Unsupported assurance
20 Mason's trough
21 Designer Cassini
22 Very, informally
23 Noble family name in medieval Italy shared by two popes
25 Mischief
27 Shot
30 Mountain near Pelion
31 Considerably, in Cannes
32 U.K. neighbor
33 Stop, in Montréal
35 They're often served with caviar
36 19th of 24
37 Ais
40 Place-kicker's aid
41 Tulip-growing center of Holland
42 "Fish Magic" and "Viaducts Break Ranks"
43 Suffer
44 More limited
45 Man ___
46 They hook up IVs
47 9-Across native
48 Rounded out?
51 "___ time"
52 Construction piece
54 "Uncle Tom's Cabin" girl
55 Westernmost of the major Hawaiian islands
58 Refractive
60 Volunteer's declaration
61 S.C. Johnson shaving gel
62 Future dr.'s exam
63 Attach, as a ribbon
64 ___-les-Moulineaux (Paris suburb)
65 "Horrors!"

DOWN

1 Massenet opera based on a Daudet novel
2 Slip
3 Ocas
4 1960s activist org.
5 Renato's wife in Verdi's "Un Ballo in Maschera"
6 Tram locale
7 Moas
8 ___ culpa
9 Eri
10 Landing place
11 At all
12 Clear, as tables
13 Abbr. on a letter to a soldier
18 Ara
22 Small songbirds
24 "Mm-hmm"
26 Take for ___
27 Ers
28 Danish astronomer who followed Copernicus
29 Children's doctor?
33 Fragrance
34 River through Köln
35 ___ nova
38 Ziggurat features
39 Slave in Buck's House of Hwang
45 Abbey Theater playwright
49 Perrier rival
50 Blade maker
51 Literary character who says "O, beware, my lord, of jealousy"
53 Major leagues, slangily, with "the"
55 Modelist's purchase
56 World champion of 1964–67, 1974–78 and 1978–79
57 Diminutive suffix
58 J.F.K. Library architect
59 "Yo te ___"

by Arthur Schulman

ACROSS

1 Former "Meet the Press" moderator Marvin
5 ___ Thule, distant unknown land
11 "___ Boys" (1886 novel)
14 Noodle product?
15 Pin-up figure?
16 Musician who started the Obscure Records label
17 Band without a drummer?
19 1989 one-man Broadway drama
20 Divine creature with six wings
21 Get in a lather
23 Rappers' posses
24 "See ya, idiot!"?
27 Goddess with a cow as an emblem
28 Corn syrup brand
29 Say again
30 "Gotta love him!"
34 N.F.L. coach Whisenhunt
35 Mission of an Army officers' school?
38 It might go for a buck
39 Having the most substance
40 Bill producers
42 Race
43 Lie idle too long
47 Nice touch from Roger Daltry and Pete Townshend?
50 Cut again
51 Concoct
52 Kenyan's neighbor
53 Small range
54 Playful kiss on the Discovery?
58 Full-screen picture, maybe: Abbr.
59 Cryptozoology figure
60 Exam with a reading comprehension section, for short
61 Orthodontist's deg.
62 Beat decisively, in slang
63 Like this puzzle . . . not!

DOWN

1 Garden gnomes and such
2 Hold fast
3 Ogler
4 Classic "S.N.L." character who spoke with rounded R's
5 Home of Arches National Park
6 Back muscle, briefly
7 It comes between dusk and dawn
8 Québec's ___ Rouleau crater
9 Rapid, to Rossini
10 Subject of an insurance investigation
11 Aids for spacewalkers
12 Torrents
13 "Let's eat!"
18 PC graphics format
22 Life time?
24 Gorge
25 1975 U.S. Open winner Manuel
26 Open galleries
28 Publisher of the fictional New York Inquirer
31 1927 E. E. Cummings play
32 Extremely, in combinations
33 '09, '10, etc.
35 Ever faithfully
36 Parts of some appliance delivery jobs
37 Quaking
38 Lallygagged
41 "MythBusters" subj.
44 Patriotic chant
45 Latin dances
46 Mazelike
48 Grps.
49 Take up again, e.g.
50 Salmon ___
52 Beloved object of 28-Down
55 "Until Every One Comes Home" grp.
56 "Not nice!"
57 One to one, for one

by Brendan Emmett Quigley

ACROSS

1 Paper carrier
8 Raised Cain
15 Heaped together
16 Element used in fire retardants
17 Something made to order?
18 With 55-Across, direction indicator
19 Women who get high?
21 Lay
22 Med. readout
25 Euripides play or its heroine
26 "Catch!"
27 Its motto is "Duty, Honor, Country"
30 Apple gadget
31 "The ___ Report"
32 Cold war grp.
34 Fast-food chain whose logo features a modified Italian flag
35 Defeated, as at a Nathan's hot dog contest
39 "___ It Time" (1977 hit)
41 Hip (to)
42 Jag
45 Cockney, e.g.
47 Been abed
48 Ship's resting place
49 "I have an idea . . ."
50 Global finance org.
51 Story that begins "All children, except one, grow up"
54 Place name popular in the 1990s
55 See 18-Across
56 "Mr. Pim Passes By" playwright
60 "The Lion in Winter" queen
61 Like penthouse suites vis-à-vis other apartments, typically

62 Melancholy
63 Picnic pest, informally

DOWN

1 Attack signal
2 Santa ___
3 Bit of art on a chest, in slang
4 Balancing pros
5 Hawaii county seat
6 Toymaking center?
7 Recliner feature
8 "Nightline" presenter
9 Sing like Andy Williams or Russ Columbo
10 ___ River, N.J.
11 Titus or Tiberius: Abbr.
12 Something needed for a change

13 Dubious
14 Nag
20 It may be red or brown
22 Series conclusions: Abbr.
23 Remote ancestor?
24 Arizona's ___ Mountains
26 Get the lead out
28 Pat of "Knute Rockne All American"
29 As such
30 Trim, as a topiary
33 Long-running TV series set in Colorado
36 Puts on
37 How to ___ knot (Boy Scout's lesson)
38 One of eight English kings, to a 45-Across

40 Could fall either way
41 Features of some sandals
42 Slanders really badly
43 Bobby's wife on "Dallas"
44 Ransacked
46 "Right you ___!"
48 Spanish kisses
51 Soul food side dish
52 Le Havre honey
53 "Well done!"
55 Split
57 Pie-eyed
58 Name tag?
59 Give all for one or one for all, e.g.?

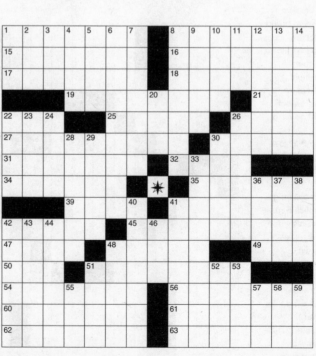

by Patrick Blindauer and Rebecca Young

ACROSS

1 ___ salad (dish with ground beef)
5 Where Panasonic is headquartered
10 Nav. ___
14 "Get ___," 1967 hit for the Esquires
15 Florida tourist destination
16 Hershey's candy
17 Like many old gym socks
18 *Baseball feat
20 ___ friends
22 Pay dirt
23 Clear, in a way
24 *Physics period
26 Garth Brooks, by birth
27 Winter Olympics races
28 Marijuana's active substance: Abbr.
29 Directional ending
30 Old greeting
31 Farm sound
32 Not just turn down
33 Repeatedly . . . and a hint to the answers to this puzzle's starred clues
37 Kind of wave
38 One of the Canterbury pilgrims
39 Golden Globe-winning English actor McShane
40 M.D.'s who deliver
41 Palm product
42 X, e.g.
46 Last word in shampoo instructions
48 *Brave front
49 Dentist's admonition
50 Do a background check on
51 "What he said"
52 *Asthmatic's concern

55 Town at one end of the Windsor Bridge
56 Something a person may take a spin in?
57 Blinded painfully
58 Filmmaker Riefenstahl
59 To be, to 33-Down
60 Targets of some sprays
61 Harriet Beecher Stowe novel

DOWN

1 They're read at services
2 Uncouth sort
3 Basilica feature
4 Hazard around an aerosol can
5 Work started by London's Philological Soc.
6 Many Mel Brooks films
7 "Dedicated to finding ___" (diabetes foundation motto)
8 Japanese port
9 The Falcons, on scoreboards
10 Cosmetician Adrien
11 Olympics venue
12 Individually, in a way
13 Leading lady
19 N.E.A. part: Abbr.
21 Part of a hazmat suit
25 Follow-up to a parent's command, maybe
26 Metal that's an effective radiation shield
28 It may be pinched
31 Range part: Abbr.
32 Treacherous expanse

33 Caligula's predecessor as emperor
34 Not gradually
35 Suffix with glee or sorrow
36 Like circus elephants
37 Potassium ___ (preservative)
41 Home of highways H-1, H-2 and H-3
42 Flap one's gums
43 Vermin hunter
44 When Romeo meets Juliet
45 Russian playwright Andreyev
47 -like
48 Insurance giant
50 ___ the Dragon, ruler of old Wallachia
53 "Yo te ___"
54 Stat for an R.B.

by Scott Atkinson

ACROSS

1 Crunched numbers
5 The Jets' retired #12
11 No. cruncher
14 Spew
15 "Aladdin" setting
16 Post-shot syllable?
17 Entertainer born 12/1/45 in 25-Across
19 Book after Galatians: Abbr.
20 Union site
21 Earliest pope to receive the title "the Great"
22 ___-à-porter
23 "High ___," 1941 film
25 Capital whose name means "sheltered bay"
27 Hammer site
28 Something to prep for
30 Rustic digs
31 In a suitable way
33 Like most customers
34 & 36 Only official residence of a reigning monarch now in the United States
37 Actress Locke of "The Heart Is a Lonely Hunter"
38 Actor Robert of "The 39 Steps"
39 Every seven days
40 With 37-Down, seven-time Wimbledon champ
41 Common pollutant
44 Measured base to peak, the world's tallest mountain
46 Los Angeles fossil site
49 Some hallucinogens, for short
50 Daughter of Cronus
52 One talking in a forest, maybe

53 Potential swimsuit embarrassment
54 Politician born 8/4/61 in 25-Across
56 Eroded, with "away"
57 Comparable with
58 ". . . ___ saw Elba"
59 Barrett of the original Pink Floyd
60 Went out, in a card game
61 Lombardy town

DOWN

1 Cheapen
2 English princess after whom a Virginia county is named
3 Nervous laugh
4 It may smell like a rose
5 "China Beach" setting
6 Relative of a husk

7 Seized the opportunity
8 More than budding
9 Marketing device
10 Guffaw syllable
11 Innocent-looking
12 Oil conduit
13 German warning
18 Drop a pop-up, say
22 Dabble in
24 Hartford-based Fortune 500 company
26 Seat of Marion County, Fla.
29 Year Caligula was assassinated
31 Priscilla and John
32 Cold comfort?
33 Talk show group
34 It's west of Davenport
35 Outdid
36 Ante destination

37 See 40-Across
38 Start of a letter to Landers
40 Look through a window, maybe
41 Five-time Kentucky Derby winner
42 Like pant legs
43 Theme of this puzzle
45 Uniform fabric
47 Te ___
48 Early tower locale
51 Opéra division
54 Do a marketing job
55 Down for the count

by Victor Fleming

ACROSS

1 It's similar to cream
5 *Jigger
10 Crawl (with)
14 '08 classmate, now
15 1967 war locale
16 Title heroine who says "One half of the world cannot understand the pleasures of the other"
17 *"That's way off"
19 Arabic for "commander"
20 1986 #1 hit for Starship
21 "Saving Grace" airer
23 "The Whiffenpoof Song" singer
24 Mideast's Mount ___
27 With 52-Across, wild guess . . . or what the answer to each starred clue has?
29 Nabokov novel
30 Stop on Magellan's circumnavigation of the world
32 Camera setting
33 Prefix denoting 10^9
35 "For real!"
38 *Photo
39 *Colorful party drink
40 *Rejected
44 Pack rat
46 El número de agosto
47 FedEx, say
49 Explorer and Navigator
51 Butt
52 See 27-Across
55 Many magicians wear them
57 QB's cry
58 Solo in science fiction

59 Nonchalance
60 Sch. located on the Rio Grande
62 *Quick hitch-up
67 Maven
68 Creating a din
69 Book before Amos
70 Give a handicap of
71 *Y-shaped item
72 ___-Aryan

DOWN

1 Suffix with Euclid
2 Trapped
3 Vegetable that's peeled
4 Shadow
5 Federal management agcy.
6 Rapper ___ Jon
7 "Is that ___?"
8 Nick name?

9 Omens
10 *What "fore" may precede
11 Daniel Decatur ___, composer of "Dixie"
12 Actor Estevez
13 San Rafael's county
18 Masculine side
22 Cuisine with sen yai noodles
24 Is seconds behind
25 Spiritualist's tool
26 Whistle-blower
28 One-up
31 Pinochle combos
34 Insect called a greenfly in Britain
36 Rat Island resident
37 Red of early jazz
41 Reason to celebrate
42 Bleached
43 Often-ladled drinks
45 Mako shark prey

47 "Shhh!," not so politely
48 Straight
50 Earned a citation?
52 Some riffraff
53 Sitar pieces
54 Small ridge on the edge of a button or dial
56 Completer of the fifth pillar of Islam
61 *Track-and-field event
63 "___ won't!"
64 Pale
65 .0000001 joule
66 Mop & ___

by Joel Fagliano

ACROSS

1 They're akin to khans
5 Punts, e.g.
10 Maintain
14 Joining of opposite sides
15 First word of the Lord's Prayer in French
16 Drop
17 ___ perpetuum (let it be everlasting)
18 Sinclair Lewis novel
20 Setting piece
22 Exotic fish
23 Venetian feature
24 Rankle
26 Series of sorties
28 Half of bi-
29 Big do
30 Tricolor pooch
34 Wind element
36 Title not acquired by Miss Spain?: Abbr.
38 ___ ring
39 Set on the court
42 Utah ski resort
45 Mass ender?
46 Gateway Arch designer
49 Made a switch in a game
52 Carriers of arms
53 Beethoven dedicatee
54 Has been around since, with "to"
57 Bomb
59 Funny Wilson
60 Went after
61 Tag words
62 "Doctor Who" villainess, with "the"
63 Italian rumbler
64 Big ados
65 Putin input?

DOWN

1 Galoots
2 Refinery products
3 Insurance company employees
4 Like some traffic
5 Suddenly break, as a twig
6 Ones examining bodies of evidence?
7 Juan's other
8 Betrays, say
9 Finish (up)
10 They're out standing in their field
11 Somewhat
12 Not natural, in a way, after "in"
13 ___ Allen furniture
19 Hold (off)
21 Coin "swallower"
25 Trunk part
26 Goddess of breezes
27 Charles and others
31 Kind of party
32 What's barely done in movies?
33 First couple's home
35 Tab, for one
37 Actor Sim who played Ebenezer Scrooge
40 1991 and 1992 U.S. Open champ
41 III in modern Rome
43 Biblical money units
44 Fleischer and others
47 It doesn't end in 00
48 Natural
49 Quit
50 Unalaska native, e.g.
51 It may precede a storm
55 Play start
56 Work on a muffler, say
58 Walk-___

by Joe Krozel

Note: When this puzzle is completed, one letter of the alphabet will appear 22 times. Shade in its square everywhere it appears. The result will be an image suggested by 36-Across.

ACROSS

1 ___ de coeur
4 Worked on
11 Ryan of "Top Gun"
14 Computer system acronym
15 Way, way back
16 Canine care grp.?
17 Tolkien creature
18 Start of a lover's quatrain
20 Big fans
22 Not straight, in a way
23 Rice-A-___
24 1950s political inits.
26 Canadian Oscar
27 Holds
29 Eur. carrier
32 Small denomination
33 ___ ante
34 Port of ancient Rome
36 1897 novel subtitled "A Grotesque Romance"
42 Composer of "The Planets"
43 True inner self
44 One way to stand
48 Fleur-de-___
49 Comparatively cockamamie
50 It's addictive
52 ___ Maj.
54 The Dakotas, once: Abbr.
55 #1 album for 13 weeks in 1966–67, with "The"
58 Where the Samoyed dog comes from
60 Eliminates undesirable parts
62 Pretense
63 According to
64 Panties, old-style
65 Pacific port where Amelia Earhart was last seen
66 Rocky point
67 Get comfortable with
68 This Across answer, appropriately

DOWN

1 Plain as day
2 Air Force base near San Antonio
3 Speak with gravity
4 It may be managed or extended
5 Ancient meeting places
6 19th-century James
7 Sugar ending
8 Filly
9 New York cardinal
10 Headwear banned by the N.F.L. in 2001
11 "Battle Cry" soldier
12 Like paradise
13 Thingumbob
19 Just manages, with "out"
21 Hindu sage
25 1973 horror flick about a doctor who turns his assistant into a cobra
28 Phnom ___
30 Having words
31 Bro or sis
34 Like unwashed hair
35 Mathematician Turing
37 TV control: Abbr.
38 Maternally related
39 Eau ___
40 Yank
41 Told tales
44 The Rum Tum Tugger, e.g.
45 New York theater on the National Register of Historic Places, with "the"
46 Like some algebra
47 1987 Suzanne Vega hit
49 Words of objection
51 Indicator of brightness
53 Astronaut's attire
56 Founded: Abbr.
57 Where the Mets once met
59 Don Juan's kiss
61 Vs.

by Patrick Blindauer

1

OGLE · JCREW · LOMA
ACER · OUIDA · ICET
FLEACIRCUS · FEAT
SEZ · ONEK · · ATARI
· FARMERSALMANAC
· · EADS · REEF ·
EHUD · · · WINNIPEG
SUPERBOWLSUNDAY
SHAVEOFF · · GARP
· · EARN · LANE ·
BULLMOOSEPARTY
ETHOS · TRES · OIS
REAP · OPENMARKET
ERSE · RENEE · BELA
TOAD · ACORN · INDY

2

ELECT · SOUSA · EYE
SITAR · APRIL · NEZ
QUALITYTIME · COP
· · SOUSE · · GILA
VAST · GODSWOUNDS
EFLATS · TIPTOES ·
IRATE · AHOLE · ·
LOVECONQUERSALL
· · HOIST · AUJUS
BARRIOS · ESPANA
SPIKEHEELS · ERAT
IPSO · QATAR · ·
DEE · GROUCHOMARX
EAR · AUDIE · NEWEL
SRS · STEPS · ENLAI

3

OTTO · SPRANG · CAD
NEON · HOAGIE · IRR
ERRS · ENFANT · GTE
SEEP · LEASES · AUS
ESSE · · ESAU · RRS
CATCHAGLIMPSEOF
· · ICU · · ETTO
LEAGUE · ERECTOR
OUGHTS · REPRESS
GRATES · ILIESCU
· AAA · · TMAC
SEEINGEYE · CONC
TOLLGATES · OKIE
RESILIENT · DENS
· TEN · · ERIS

Clues with errors: 1-, 14-, 19- and 24-Across, and 8-, 9-, 28-, 47-, 49- and
50-Down

4

RIAL · STYX · HALAS
ESTA · EAVE · ALAMO
CIT[YSL]ICKER · RADII
UNLOOSES · CHR[YSL]ER
STEWS · SALAMI ·
EOE · SCALAR · PTS
· FASHION · EPIC
PIGLATIN · GRETA
ANAIS · TIREIRON
COLT · COLOGNE ·
ENL · SATANS · CAR
· ERESTU · AKITA
PA[YSL]IPS · RESPECTS
APACT · BEAUT[YSL]EEP
LEVEE · ANTE · ORNE
EXERT · ITSY · TODD

5

CEST · SLIM · PAVES
UTAH · TIKI · ELIOT
PELE · EVEN · NORSE
PROOFREADINNG ·
ENO · OLD · SEEING
DENALI · PAM · NEA
· MINTER · TAILS
· TYPOGRPAHICAL
CROSS · ESTEEM ·
DOS · SKI · DREAMS
STEREO · AGO · MAE
· MISPELLEDWORD
ALIST · NOOR · HERA
LATKE · OCHO · ABET
THESE · SHAW · MADE

6

```
BADE  SPLIT  FORE
AMEX  PLAZA  IPOD
RULE  RAZOR  GELS
BLACKEYEDPEARY
SEN  NEE  SERAPE
 TONE  RTS  NOTON
  IAM  HIM  OLD
 GOLDENARCHERY
RAN  TIN  SAG
ELENI  BEG  SOLD
CAPONS  EAT  IUM
 CORDUROYPANTRY
STUD  MORSE  ACHE
MINI  POSER  SHAY
ACDC  STORY  TIME
```

7

```
CURE  BELLE  SPAR
ITAL  ORIEL  PINA
RUNG  LILAC  LENT
CRINKLE  PRAISES
ANNAN  ATILT
 IOTAS  CASABA
WHIRLIGIG  LAG
RATTLER  EPISTLE
ERA  ARTICHOKE
NETTLE  MANIA
 WORDS  EPSOM
LORELAI  SPREADS
AMIE  UNITY  SUED
VEST  QATAR  UNTO
ONES  SHONE  PASS
```

8

```
MAKO  FLESH  WORF
ALEX  EULER  ELAL
DUMBULLETS  LADY
EMPORIUM  ELFIN
 WINSITUATION
CROSSE  OTTO
HER  IRONEDOUT
ONCEISNOTENOUGH
POSTDATES  THE
 EINE  PLEASE
CHIRODRIGUEZ
HASNT  DIRTPOOR
ALLI  RAINGOAWAY
SEAT  ATONE  SIRE
MYMY  EMMYS  SESS
```

9

```
WORSHIP  TAMALES
BROCADE  EMINENT
CROONER  CANTATA
 TOOMUCHHEAVEN
MUFTI  OIL  INT
OTO  FIFE  MOTTO
WEREWOLF  AUSTEN
 RAREEARTH
STMARK  EPITAPHS
ARISE  SPED  HAI
CAN  MAO  SCAMP
HIGHWAYTOHELL
ENLARGE  RADIATE
TEENIER  CHANNEL
SEDATES  ANNEXES
```

10

```
ABAA  AMAT  MSGS
LEIGH  DOTO  ATIT
TONEITDOWN  MESA
 RUNNINGONEMPTY
 CTN  EROS
DARYA  DJS  ATTEN
ERE  THROWITHOME
NODS  IONIC  SOAR
TOOTHENAMEL  LIV
EMCEE  ESS  AISLE
 TMAN  ADM
CHOCTAWINDIANS
LOBE  GOLDENMEAN
OPEL  ARIA  GABLE
GIRL  TEAK  NOTE
```

11

```
THOR   JOEY   SCALD
SINE   ARLO   EULER
KEEP   CUMULATIVE
   LEAK    RIC   MEA
EMIGRATE    SOMBER
MENSCLUB    LAI
ETE    SNO   ESKERS
NORSE   ANG   TENET
DOSING   IOS    TSU
   TSO   COMPLAIN
ROTUND   SPOILING
ICH   ABA   LEAL
PROGRESSED   NIKE
EERIE   HERE   ONIT
RANTS   YEAR   SGTS
```

The circled letters, rearranged, spell EMPTY

12

```
KAMPALA   TVSTARS
AREARUG   RATATAT
VISCERA   ICINESS
ADHESIVEBAND
      RODEO   TOADS
SSRS   NSA   ODEA
UTE   MASSTHERAPY
SAC   ASP   UMA   GAY
SPORTSCOVER   IRE
ELIE   TAN   COTS
XENIA   CRUSH
   GARBDISPOSAL
JEANNIE   DIORAMA
ACTEDAS   ENRAGED
BOLDEST   AGELESS
```

13

```
CADS   CHAD   CREST
AWOL   RARE   ROYCE
GAZA   EGOS   ICEAX
EYECLAUDIUS   TNT
   KITE   ANIGH
SLEEVE   CRISPER
WAYNE   SANO   OJAI
APE   SOPRANO   UNC
PELE   LODZ   SPREE
LISTENS   STAYED
   KLEIG   POET
AWE   ANEYEFORANI
SHIPS   BUTT   OREO
PEKOE   OLEO   LEAN
STEER   BERN   SALS
```

14

```
THORN   ITINA   DDE
RELEE   DECIS   ION
AUDIO   LEISURELY
PRESCIENCE   HULA
PERSON   ALITY
   UNCAGE   OMEGA
DUKE   HRE   IDEALS
ONE   SEC   OND   CUE
ZIPPED   SRS   SHEA
EXTRA   TUKTUK
   INFIN   ITIVES
AHEM   ANDALUSIAN
ROYALTIES   RUNTO
THE   CHECK   NICER
SOD   DARKS   STENT
```

15

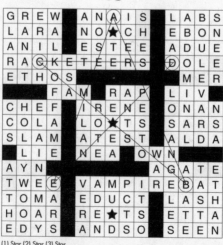

```
GREW   ANAIS   LABS
LARA   NOCH   EBON
ANIL   ESTEE   ADUE
RACKETEERS   DOLE
ETHOS        MER
   FAM   RAP   LIV
CHEF   IRENE   ONAN
COLA   LOTS   SARS
SLAM   ATEST   ALDA
   LIE   NEA   OWN
AYN        AGATE
TWEE   VAMPIREBAT
TOMA   EDUCT   LASH
HOAR   RETS   ETTA
EDYS   ANDSO   SEEN
```

(1) Star (2) Star (3) Star

16

```
D E B R A ■ F A R S I ■ O A F
A R E E D ■ I C E I N ■ D R J
W I N D O W S H A D E ■ E T O
G Q T Y P E ■ E L E V A T O R
■ ■ E T D S ■ B E G O O D ■ ■
L A X ■ E S Q ■ R A R E ■ ■
I L I V E ■ U S E R ■ N O S E
A T N O ■ L A P P S ■ D A W N
R E G T ■ O T R A ■ D A R I N
■ ■ I P O S ■ I N N ■ S T E
S L O V A K ■ R O A M ■ ■
S I N E W A V E ■ A L C O V E
T E C ■ S T O C K M A R K E T
A B U ■ A M T O O ■ B A I R N
R Y E ■ T E E N S ■ S E E Y A
```

17

```
P U T T ■ R I P ■ P O L I S H
E S A I ■ I D A ■ O P E N T O
R E C E I P T S ■ S T E F A N
■ ■ G R E A S E ■ I L E N E
T O G A E ■ G E T S C A R D S
A L U M N U S ■ H E A ■ S S T
C A R E E R ■ H E E L ■ ■
O N U S ■ S T I R S ■ A B B E
■ ■ L U I S ■ A R T E R Y
S A C ■ A L E ■ S W A T T E R
P U L L S A G U N ■ I R A T E
U B O A T ■ S P A R T A ■ ■
R U S H I N ■ S K E T C H E S
G R E T N A ■ E E G ■ T I V O
E N S I G N ■ T D S ■ S P E D
```

18

```
R A V E N ■ S C A T ■ R E A D
U P O N E ■ T U B A ■ I P S E
B A T T W I R L E R ■ L I S P
I C E ■ S M U T ■ D E C O R
K E R O U A C ■ T R O U N C E
■ ■ P I C K Y O U R P O I S
A S S E T ■ A N N A ■ V A S
W A N D ■ G A N G S ■ F E T E
A T A ■ D O W N ■ D A L E S
Y U K T E R R I T O R Y ■ ■
G R E E L E Y ■ A M O E B A S
A D E N I ■ P R E P ■ O N T
M A Y O ■ B R A I N S U R G E
E Y E R ■ C A L F ■ I N A I R
S S S S ■ C H E F ■ N I X O N
```

19

```
A C D C ■ A M W A Y ■ H M O
S H O E ■ C U R B S ■ B O E R
P [IMP] L Y ■ A N I S E ■ L Y R A
■ L O N G T E R M [IMP] A C T
S K [IMP] O N ■ B I N ■ O S S I E
T R A N S ■ E N T E R ■ ■
E A S E ■ S A G ■ S E T U P S
M I S S I O N [IMP] O S S I B L E
S T E E D S ■ L B O ■ G O A T
■ Y O D E L ■ [IMP] E A C H
G R A I L ■ E M I ■ E R T E S
L I T T L E D E V I L S ■
[IMP] A L E ■ B U N I N ■ H E E L
S L A M ■ A C T O N ■ R A G U
E S S ■ ■ Y E S N O ■ [IMP] R O V
```

20

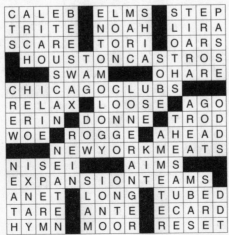

```
C A L E B ■ E L M S ■ S T E P
T R I T E ■ N O A H ■ L I R A
S C A R E ■ T O R I ■ O A R S
■ H O U S T O N C A S T R O S
■ ■ S W A M ■ ■ O H A R E
C H I C A G O C L U B S ■ ■
R E L A X ■ L O O S E ■ A G O
E R I N ■ D O N N E ■ T R O D
W O E ■ R O G G E ■ A H E A D
■ ■ N E W Y O R K M E A T S
N I S E I ■ ■ A I M S ■ ■
E X P A N S I O N T E A M S
A N E T ■ L O N G ■ T U B E D
T A R E ■ A N T E ■ E C A R D
H Y M N ■ M O O R ■ R E S E T
```

21

HOS ▪ OFT ▪ RIPTORN
ANTACID ▪ ITERATE
WEEPERS ▪ BERATED
KAPPAS ▪ EMIL ▪
▪ FANTASY ▪ ALOT
OVALS ▪ SPECULATE
BITS ▪ CII ▪ FLARES
ISH ▪ PHANTOM ▪ RLS
STEELE ▪ OAS ▪ PYLE
PARTYFOUL ▪ SOHOS
OSSO ▪ ATLANTA ▪
▪ ISAK ▪ VIAGRA
TELLALL ▪ BATSMEN
SPEEDEE ▪ ENCHANT
PATSDRY ▪ NTH ▪ NOS

22

BOSC ▪ FOLKS ▪ ELMO
ARCO ▪ ADIEU ▪ AEON
RIOS ▪ DOMES ▪ CFOS
NORTHERNLIGHTS ▪
SNEAD ▪ SEATO ▪
▪ STREP ▪ LIVID
PIT ▪ VIDEOCAMERA
ASEA ▪ GUSTO ▪ ERAT
CLASSACTION ▪ SSE
EARTH ▪ OSTER ▪
▪ SEUSS ▪ DENTS
DIRECTORSSHOUT
TONI ▪ ROMEO ▪ ALTA
ARTS ▪ ARIAS ▪ BIER
IMOK ▪ METRO ▪ SEEK

23

SUIT ▪ GLEAM ▪ CA⑨
ANNO ▪ RATIO ▪ MOST
MP③PLAYERS ▪ OLIO
LCD ▪ ASS ▪ BESTOF⑤
▪ UNPOPULAR ▪
⑧MAN ▪ VAS ▪ LIDS
⑥SHOOTER ▪ VENEER
IDO ▪ WORⓀ②④⑦ ▪ REO
TOYING ▪ SYSTEMIC
▪ SSNS ▪ APE ▪ TANK
▪ SURFⒶAREA ▪
SCRAPER ▪ REV ▪ ORG
WHEN ▪ LATOYAⒿSON
AIDE ▪ EMILE ▪ USTA
MCⓆ ▪ TENDS ▪ PA⑩T

Ⓐ=Ace, Ⓚ=King, Ⓠ=Queen, Ⓙ=Jack

24

LEICA ▪ HONG ▪ SCUD
EⓍCEL ▪ EMIR ▪ CINE
SPERM ▪ ROTO ▪ ANDA
TICTACTOEWINNER
ERA ▪ NEZ ▪ TATARS
REPEAL ▪ JOHN ▪ MDI
▪ MCLEAN ▪ MOOR
▪ POISONWARNING ▪
CANT ▪ DENIAL ▪
OME ▪ PROD ▪ GISELE
SPLISH ▪ BEL ▪ MAⓍ
THIRTYINOLDROME
ULNA ▪ TRAⓍ ▪ OATER
MEET ▪ HAZE ▪ WREST
ETRE ▪ MEIR ▪ NESTS

25

WOLFF ▪ WAIL ▪ SHAD
AKIRA ▪ ALTO ▪ HIFI
CAPITALISM ▪ ONTO
▪ CAPN ▪ ABRADED
▪ WITHOUTFAILURE
RANI ▪ STEARNS ▪
ITSOK ▪ LCDS ▪ MEN
TEENAGE ▪ TIEPINS
ART ▪ BOTH ▪ SACRE
▪ FUNERAL ▪ KROC
ISLIKERELIGION
RAELIAN ▪ TARS ▪
ANGE ▪ WITHOUTSIN
BEAR ▪ OTOE ▪ NAFTA
URLS ▪ LYRA ▪ TNOTE

26

C	L	I	M	B	■	I	S	L	A	■	R	A	G	S
C	A	N	O	E	■	S	T	A	R	T	E	D	U	P
L	U	T	E	S	■	A	U	S	T	R	A	L	I	A
E	R	E	■	T	R	A	C	T	■	O	P	A	L	S
F	A	S	T	B	U	C	K	■	C	U	P	I	D	■
■	T	E	E	M	■	O	R	A	T	E	■			
T	W	I	X	T	■	I	N	O	N	■	A	H	A	B
H	A	N	■	S	E	C	E	D	E	■	R	O	S	E
A	X	E	L	■	R	E	S	I	S	T	■	R	E	V
N	Y	S	E	■	N	U	N	N	■	E	S	S	A	Y
■	G	R	I	P	E	■	W	A	K	E	■			
■	B	R	A	H	E	■	C	H	E	M	I	S	T	S
P	A	U	L	Y	■	A	K	E	E	M	■	H	I	E
A	S	I	A	M	I	N	O	R	■	A	B	O	D	E
G	I	N	G	E	R	N	U	T	■	T	R	E	A	D
E	L	S	E	■	K	A	T	Z	■	E	A	R	L	Y

27

S	S	W	■	A	H	E	A	P	■	S	A	L	U	T
A	Q	I	■	D	U	T	C	H	■	I	R	I	S	H
D	U	N	■	D	E	C	K	O	F	F	I	C	E	R
D	E	E	P	L	Y	■	N	E	T	Z	E	R	O	■
E	L	B	E	■	V	I	E	W	S	■	N	I	B	■
S	C	A	L	L	I	O	N	■	S	D	S	■		
T	H	R	O	A	T	L	O	Z	E	N	G	E	■	
■	S	I	E	G	■	E	N	Y	O	■				
■	A	I	R	M	A	I	L	L	E	T	T	E	R	■
I	S	M	■	M	I	S	S	H	A	P	E	■		
M	B	A	■	D	I	M	A	G	■	A	K	I	M	■
B	A	T	C	A	V	E	■	C	O	M	E	T	O	■
A	R	E	A	C	O	D	E	M	A	P	■	O	A	R
C	R	U	S	H	■	I	L	O	S	E	■	U	P	S
K	O	R	E	A	■	C	L	E	A	R	■	T	H	E

28

↵	P	I	K	E	■	I	L	S	A	■	O	W	E	S
K	I	R	I	N	■	O	A	K	S	■	K	O	N	A
E	L	E	N	A	■	T	W	I	S	T	A	N	D	↵
Y	O	N	■	B	R	A	D	B	U	R	Y	■		
■	T	E	S	L	A	■	Y	O	R	E	■	J	A	W
■	W	E	D	S	■	B	E	S	E	E	C	H	■	
M	A	K	E	S	A	U	↵	■	S	A	L	T	Y	■
E	G	A	D	■	R	E	↵	E	D	■	S	L	I	M
R	A	Z	E	R	■	↵	T	O	S	T	O	N	E	■
L	I	O	N	E	S	S	■	A	W	O	L	■		
E	N	O	■	T	O	O	K	■	S	P	A	I	N	■
■	S	I	N	C	E	R	E	R	■	C	A	T	■	
↵	I	N	G	P	O	I	N	T	■	A	L	A	M	O
U	N	I	T	■	R	A	Y	E	■	N	E	M	E	A
P	A	L	S	■	A	L	A	S	■	O	V	E	R	↵

29

C	B	S	■	F	A	C	E	D	■	A	J	I	F	F
L	O	O	■	I	R	O	N	Y	■	R	A	D	I	I
U	N	D	E	R	C	O	V	E	R	A	G	E	N	T
B	E	A	N	■	S	L	Y	■	A	B	U	S	E	S
■	V	I	I	I	■	A	R	I	A	■				
■	S	W	O	R	N	T	O	S	E	C	R	E	C	Y
S	H	E	I	K	■	H	I	S	■	S	L	O	E	■
E	E	L	■	S	A	B	B	A	T	H	■	A	H	A
M	A	L	A	■	B	O	O	■	A	S	T	E	R	■
I	F	I	T	O	L	D	Y	O	U	T	H	E	N	■
■	P	L	A	Y	■	F	R	E	E	■				
D	E	C	E	I	T	■	I	F	S	■	L	A	M	P
I	D	H	A	V	E	T	O	K	I	L	L	Y	O	U
E	D	U	C	E	■	O	W	E	N	S	■	E	L	M
T	A	M	E	S	■	R	A	Y	E	D	■	S	E	A

30

C	L	A	S	P	■	S	K	A	■	M	A	D	A	M
R	I	F	L	E	■	A	I	L	■	A	L	E	R	O
A	A	R	O	N	■	C	L	A	S	S	I	C	A	L
B	R	O	W	N	B	R	O	N	C	O	C	O	L	T
■	P	E	R	U	■	A	R	N	E	■				
L	O	C	O	■	A	M	P	L	E	■	S	C	A	M
O	S	A	K	A	■	I	D	E	A	■	A	G	E	■
C	H	I	E	F	T	E	X	A	N	S	A	I	N	T
H	E	R	■	L	U	C	E	■	P	U	R	E	E	■
S	A	N	K	■	N	O	L	A	N	■	T	O	W	S
■	A	S	I	T	■	L	E	G	O	■				
G	I	A	N	T	C	O	W	B	O	Y	B	I	L	L
N	O	T	S	O	S	U	R	E	■	R	A	D	I	O
U	N	M	A	N	■	R	E	D	■	O	H	A	R	A
S	A	S	S	Y	■	S	N	O	■	S	N	E	A	D

31

```
T R O T   S A H L   I N B A D
H A Z E   O L A Y   N O O N E
O N O N E S O W N   N S Y N C
R U N A R O U N D S U E Z
O P E N T O   A W E   I T A
    T E N O F   E N G I R D
S I B     M A C A D A M I A
P L A Y S H A R D T O G E T Z
A L L A T O N C E     N E E
S E T T E R   E F I L E
M R I   P A P   D O N N I E
    C L A S S I F I E D A D Z
R E S E W   H O L D W A T E R
A R E N A   A T O I   L E N A
H E A D Y   W A R T   L S T S
```

32

```
F A D E S   F L A W   A M O S
E C O L E   I O T A   D I L L
S H O O T S T A R S   O N L Y
S E R I A L   E N D   T I E
    S T O C K S T U F F E R
G I B E   W H I T   B O A
A B A   L I O N   D O R M S
S E R V E S U G G E S T I O N
  T E E T H   P A V E   L I E
    D I S   F I N I   P Y L E
S W I N G S I N G L E S
H A T   O I L   L A Y M A N
E X A M   S L I D E S C A L E
R E L O   Q U I D   T H R O E
I D L E   O P I E   S E X E D
```

33

```
B E G O R R A   S P R   P A T
A R A B I A N   E S O B E S O
J O S E P H I   N E B A K E R
A S H Y     S U B L E T S
    E B B S   E D E L
M A N D A R I   N O R A N G E
A K A   R E N T   D O R M
Y E O   B R E A K I N   H E P
E L M O   Z E N O   O T T
R A I N R A I   N G O A W A Y
    R U I N   S A K I
S E S A M E S     S L I M
S T U M B L I   N G B L O C K
G A L P A L S   S U R E B E T
T S K   S O T   A M A S S E S
```

34

```
B O Z O   I C O N S   E G G [HEAD]
I L E T   N O H O W   P A L O
G A R E   C N O T E   I R O N
[HEAD] F O R T H E H I L L S
E I E I O     P L A C A R D
D I S   Y U A N [HEAD] T O T O E
    B O S N I A   P A T E
S H R U N K E N H E A D S
G H I A   A C T U A L
R A D I O [HEAD] E S T S   S O B
E W E N E C K   E A T M E
    D R A W B R I D G E A [HEAD]
A N T E   S I R E N   L E H I
X E N A   E K I N G   E L A N
[HEAD] E N D   S E G U E   T E N G
```

35

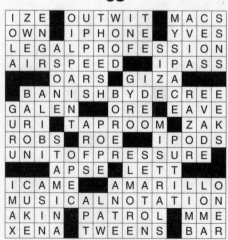

```
I Z E   O U T W I T   M A C S
O W N   I P H O N E   Y V E S
L E G A L P R O F E S S I O N
A I R S P E E D   I P A S S
      O A R S   G I Z A
  B A N I S H B Y D E C R E E
G A L E N   O R E   E A V E
U R I   T A P R O O M   Z A K
R O B S   R O E   I P O D S
U N I T O F P R E S S U R E
    A P S E   L E T T
I C A M E   A M A R I L L O
M U S I C A L N O T A T I O N
A K I N   P A T R O L   M M E
X E N A   T W E E N S   B A R
```

36

G	O	F	A	R	■	I	N	A	P	T	■	C	L	V
E	R	A	T	O	■	N	A	D	E	R	■	R	A	E
T	E	N	E	T	■	J	A	M	I	E	F	O	X	X
■	■	T	I	C	T	A	C	■	E	L	S	I	E	■
J	E	A	N	■	R	I	P	E	R	■	A	S	T	R
E	A	S	T	■	A	L	I	C	I	A	K	E	Y	S
T	R	I	O	S	■	M	O	O	S	E	■	■	■	■
S	P	A	■	A	S	H	A	N	T	I	■	S	O	Y
■	■	K	L	I	E	G	■	■	S	E	P	I	A	■
D	E	L	L	A	R	E	E	S	E	■	P	I	L	L
I	D	E	E	■	S	L	A	T	E	■	S	K	Y	E
A	G	A	I	N	■	W	I	L	L	I	E	■	■	■
B	E	R	N	I	E	M	A	C	■	A	L	L	O	Y
L	I	N	■	C	L	E	R	K	■	N	O	E	N	D
O	N	S	■	K	I	N	D	S	■	K	N	E	E	S

37

A	G	R	A	■	C	R	A	B	■	C	H	O	K	E
W	E	A	N	■	N	I	L	E	■	H	O	T	E	L
O	R	I	G	I	N	O	F	S	P	E	C	I	E	S
L	E	N	I	N	■	A	T	O	M	■	S	P	A	■
■	S	N	E	A	K	■	I	N	L	A	■	■	■	■
■	C	H	A	R	L	E	S	R	D	A	R	W	I	N
P	L	O	■	T	A	R	T	■	B	E	A	M	E	■
A	I	W	A	■	S	N	A	C	K	■	A	F	E	W
S	M	E	L	T	■	H	O	E	S	■	F	A	T	■
A	B	R	A	H	A	M	L	I	N	C	O	L	N	■
■	N	E	R	O	■	L	O	R	R	E	■	■	■	■
O	K	S	■	A	A	R	E	■	A	N	I	S	E	■
R	E	P	U	B	L	I	C	A	N	P	A	R	T	Y
B	R	O	N	C	■	T	R	O	Y	■	T	O	L	E
S	I	T	E	S	■	Z	U	L	U	■	E	N	O	S

38

T	M	A	N	■	E	M	I	L	■	O	H	J	O	Y
J	E	R	I	■	Y	O	D	A	■	B	U	E	N	O
M	A	R	M	■	E	B	A	Y	W	I	N	D	O	W
A	G	E	O	F	■	H	U	H	S	■	■	■	■	■
X	R	A	Y	O	F	H	O	P	E	■	L	I	V	E
X	E	R	■	C	I	A	■	E	V	O	K	E	D	■
■	■	T	U	R	B	A	N	L	E	G	E	N	D	■
C	B	E	R	S	■	L	I	E	■	T	O	A	D	Y
R	A	D	I	O	S	A	M	I	G	O	S	■	■	■
U	R	G	E	N	T	■	N	N	E	■	A	M	E	■
Z	E	E	S	■	A	W	E	S	C	R	A	V	E	N
■	■	D	R	A	X	■	S	Q	U	A	D	■	■	■
E	X	T	R	A	E	X	T	R	A	■	U	L	N	A
M	Y	B	A	D	■	E	O	N	S	■	A	S	I	S
O	Z	A	W	A	■	S	L	A	P	■	S	E	T	H

39

J	O	K	E	■	P	L	I	E	D	■	B	A	J	A
E	V	I	L	■	L	O	R	C	A	■	E	X	E	C
W	A	R	E	■	A	N	A	R	T	■	A	L	E	E
■	L	I	V	I	N	G	Q	U	A	R	T	E	R	S
■	E	M	O	■	S	O	I	■	■	■	■	■	■	■
B	U	R	N	I	N	G	Q	U	E	S	T	I	O	N
A	T	E	A	T	■	L	U	S	T	Y	■	L	X	I
T	E	A	M	■	B	O	A	T	S	■	S	E	E	K
C	R	I	■	E	R	A	S	E	■	S	A	N	Y	O
H	O	M	E	C	O	M	I	N	G	Q	U	E	E	N
■	L	O	U	■	A	F	C	■	■	■	■	■	■	■
S	T	R	I	N	G	Q	U	A	R	T	E	T	S	■
T	W	I	X	■	H	U	R	L	S	■	P	R	E	Z
L	O	C	I	■	A	A	L	T	O	■	A	U	R	A
O	D	O	R	■	M	Y	S	O	N	■	N	E	A	P

40

■	C	A	N	A	D	A	■	D	E	F	A	M	E	■
■	O	N	E	L	A	P	■	R	A	D	A	M	E	S
■	B	E	W	A	R	E	■	S	A	N	G	R	I	A	S
■	■	S	I	D	E	L	I	N	E	D	■	■	■	■
■	P	A	R	K	A	■	L	E	S	E	■	I	M	A	X
■	I	D	E	A	■	U	D	D	E	R	■	S	O	R	E
■	E	M	A	N	A	T	E	D	■	A	T	L	A	S
■	■	I	D	I	T	A	R	O	D	T	R	A	I	L	■
■	I	R	E	N	E	■	G	O	O	D	N	E	S	S
■	C	A	R	T	■	S	E	R	G	E	■	T	R	E	Y
■	E	L	S	E	■	C	R	A	M	■	S	P	E	A	R
■	■	R	O	O	T	C	A	N	A	L	■	■	■	■
■	P	E	D	I	G	R	E	E	■	O	N	A	J	A	G
■	O	R	I	O	L	E	S	■	R	E	C	E	D	E
■	P	E	E	R	E	D	■	A	R	E	T	O	O

41

```
A C N E _ C A N C E L _ S A P
C O A X _ O V I E D O _ H S T
C O U[PED]E V I L L E S _ A H A
U P S I D E S _ E N T I R E _
S U E T S _ Q B S _ S[PED]B Y
E P E E _ A S U _ M A G O O
_ S A L T I N E S _ E R R
S S T _ P E D X I N G _ D O E
U N A _ A R S O N I S T _
B I[PED]A L _ T E D _ O D I N
S T E M _ S T E _ G R E C O
_ C L A M M Y _ T H I N A I R
S H A _ C A[PED]C R U S A D E R
K E Y _ C R U S E S _ D E S I
I D S _ I M P I S H _ O R T S
```

42

```
L I M I T _ S H I E R _ I N T
E N O K I _ K A T I E _ N O R
G R E E N W I T H N V _ D R E
S E N S E I _ P A S S B O O K
_ A S P I C _ R O O S
N E P O R T I N A S T O R M
S W A P _ E N S _ U R N
C E L E B R E _ A L Y S S A S
_ R O I _ A T E _ O H I O
_ M E A W A R D W I N N E R S
S O W N _ A R O M A _
W H I T E L I E _ A G G I E S
I A N _ R U N N I N G O N M T
P I G _ O C E A N _ E R N I E
E R S _ S I D L E _ R E S T S
```

43

```
C O R K _ G O L E M _ E L A L
O R A N _ A S O N E _ N O M E
M A N O _ L L O Y D _ T W I G
A L I T T L E M A D N E S S
_ T I E R S _ L E N
A D D S T O _ D E A D S E A
N O R _ I N T H E S P R I N G
T W A S _ H A M _ E X O N
I S W H O L E S O M E _ E R E
C E L A D O N _ A L A R M S
_ K I A _ T U C K S
_ E V E N F O R T H E K I N G
A V I S _ E M O T E _ O D O R
M E N U _ R I V E T _ U L N A
P R E P _ S T E R E _ T E E M
```

44

```
J E W _ C H I R P _ W I G G Y
U V A _ B A N D O _ S N A R E
G A R Y G Y G A X _ J A S O N
_ O B I E _ N O G S
C A G Y _ N A P S _ E E L
O L E O _ G R A N D P R I X
M E N S A _ T I R O _ N Y M
E K E _ G O R E T E X _ E L O
T E R _ A N I L _ Y A T E S
_ G A G R E F L E X _ B A N E
_ T E N _ F A N G _ E X E S
G A I T _ D A T A _
I L O S T _ G U M M O M A R X
V E N T I _ A K E E M _ P I X
E X X O N _ T E N S E _ B O X
```

45

```
J U D Y _ C L A D _ N O V A
O P I E _ R U B E _ A B E L
A T T S _ M I N I M O Z A R T
D O Z I N G B A T _ R A M B O
_ D U M _ N O R A S _
C A R O M _ S E R E N E
U T E _ B O O Z Y W O N D E R
J O N I _ S N I D E _ E A V E
O Z O N E L I N E R S _ D I A
_ S L I C E R _ P S A L M
_ B R O W N _ A R C
C R I M E _ C O Z Y Y O U N G
L I O N S D O Z E N _ T R O T
A N T I _ O O Z E _ I S S O
M E S A _ S P Y S _ A A H S
```

46

```
O H O H ■ B A S S ■ A R N E L
K E N O ■ E T C H ■ V O I L A
S H O W E D T H E D O C T O R
■ ■ S A R A ■ L E N ■ R H O
N O M O R E ■ E L L ■ L O I S
A N A ■ S A X ■ T R A U M A
D I R E C T S T R A I T S ■
A N K L E ■ E R A ■ E T A I L
■ M O N I C A S E L E C T S
C R Y P T S ■ C A N ■ I S A
I O W E ■ S O T ■ G O O D A T
N G O ■ C U Z ■ F I R S ■
E U R O P E A N U N C T I O N
M E D A L ■ W A R E ■ E N D O
A S S T S ■ A M Y S ■ O N E D
```

47

```
L E A D ■ P A T H ■ O M A N I
O N C E ■ O S H A ■ A U T O S
G O D F A T H E R O F S O U L
E S C A P E ■ M D L ■ E R S E
■ C E N T ■ U S S ■
F E D E X C O M P E T I T O R
R R R ■ Y E A ■ N A V A H O
A R O M A ■ D Y E ■ T E N A M
N O N A M E ■ A N O ■ G R E
C L E V E L A N D P L A Y E R
■ S I R ■ S P I N ■
G I G S ■ Z A P ■ O N C A L L
I V Y L E A G U E S C H O O L
B O R E R ■ O N M E ■ O K E D
B R O W N ■ N Y P D ■ R I B S
```

48

```
A D D L E ■ O T S ■ M T G E
Q U E U E S ■ K H A R T O U M
U B A N G I ■ R U M I N A N T
A L F A ■ B E A M E D ■
S I T ■ D E M ■ B A G H D A D
■ N O C A R B S ■ S E E Y O U
■ O R I A N A ■ F E N D
C A P I T A L O F F E N S E S
O P E N ■ M O R A L E ■
S A R O N G ■ P A N A R A B
T R I P O L I ■ M A N ■ S E P
■ F I D G E T ■ A S I A
S P A C E B A R ■ I N B O R N
N E W D E L H I ■ C I R R U S
L A W S ■ Y O N ■ B A T T Y
```

49

```
Ⓞ S T E R ■ A W E I N S P I Ⓞ
L O R R E ■ N E U R O P A T H
I M A M S ■ T A L K R A D I O
N A M A T H ■ R E I D ■ U N U
E S S ■ A D A R N ■ M A A R
■ J U R E ■ G A Y ■
P R O U D P A P A ■ F R O D O
R O U N D S T H E C O R N E R
E E R I E ■ H I S O R H E R S
■ O R I ■ O D E S ■
S T A R ■ N A P P Y ■ A N C
I R S ■ S A V E ■ S I T F O R
Z E P P E L I N S ■ T H O R O
E V I C T I O N S ■ C R U M P
Ⓞ I N T H E N E W ■ H U L A Ⓞ
```

Note: The O's in the corners represent HOOP, RING, CIRCLE and ZERO, each used twice.

50

```
P A R T I E S ■ E A R T I P S
I N A R O M P ■ A L I E N E E
R E T I N O L ■ C A N A S T A
A M T ■ S T A S H E D ■ A N T
T O L D ■ E T C ■ S O N A R
E N E R O ■ R I G ■ S E M I
S E R O W ■ J A D E ■ P R E P
■ P E R I M E T E R ■
A M A S ■ A B B A ■ L E D U P
P O M E ■ G E L ■ M Y R N A
R U N T S ■ E G O ■ S O N S
I R E ■ T H E S A M E ■ V E T
E N S U R E D ■ S A L I E R I
S E I Z I N G ■ U N B R A V E
T R A I P S E ■ P I A S T E R
```

51

A	B	C		A	G	R	E	E	D		C	L	U	E
B	R	O		P	U	E	N	T	E		H	E	N	S
B	A	R	N	E	Y	F	I	E	F		A	R	C	S
A	N	N	E		S	S	A		R	E	S	O	L	E
		B	O	W		C	O	A	L	M	I	E	N	
T	O	R	N	O	U	T		N	Y	U				
S	N	E	A	K	P	E	K	E		L	I	F	E	R
A	M	A	T		S	C	O	U	R		N	I	T	E
R	Y	D	E	R		H	A	P	P	Y	F	E	T	E
			O	B	I		S	I	M	I	L	E	S	
S	N	O	W	C	O	E	N		A	D	D			
C	U	B	I	S	M		A	E	R		E	M	M	A
A	R	A	L		B	O	R	D	E	R	L	I	E	N
B	S	M	T		A	R	C	A	N	A		C	A	T
S	E	A	S		Y	E	S	M	E	N		E	L	S

52

C	A	L	M		S	O	U	S	A		T	W	O	S
A	L	E	E		A	G	R	E	E		A	R	U	T
P	A	G	E	T	U	R	N	E	R		K	I	T	E
I	M	I	T	A	T	E		R	O	G	E	T	S	
T	E	R		L	E	S	S		S	U	I	T	O	R
A	D	O	R	E	S		E	F	T	S		E	L	I
L	A	N	E	S		B	R	E	A		O	N	E	G
		G	E	T	O	V	E	R	I	T				
L	I	M	O		H	O	E	D		R	O	S	S	I
O	C	A		M	E	N	U		B	R	E	T	O	N
B	E	G	E	T	S		P	A	R	E		U	M	W
	B	I	T	M	A	P		S	A	G	E	T	E	A
B	E	L	A		I	N	Q	U	I	S	I	T	O	R
M	E	L	T		N	E	A	R	S		R	E	N	D
I	R	A	S		T	U	T	E	E		E	R	E	S

53

	H	A	M	L	E	T		D	E	I	S	T	S	
P	O	S	T	U	R	E		R	E	S	O	R	T	S
I	N	T	A	I	L	S		A	L	L	R	I	S	E
C	O	O	P	S		T	A	W		A	B	B	I	E
A	R	L	O		F	S	L	I	C		S	U	M	P
R	E	A		A	L	I	E	N	O	R		T	O	E
D	E	T	O	N	A	T	E		L	E	G	E	N	D
			P	E	T	E		R	O	S	E			
H	I	T	S	A	T		M	O	R	E	L	A	N	D
E	O	E		R	A	R	E	B	I	T		I	E	R
A	D	M	S		X	E	N	O	N		A	L	A	E
P	I	P	E	T		C	U	T		I	G	E	T	A
E	D	U	A	R	D	O		I	G	N	O	R	E	D
D	E	R	N	I	E	R		C	I	T	R	O	N	S
	S	A	S	S	E	D		S	L	O	A	N	S	

54

A	T	E	S	T		R	A	G		I	R	K	S		S	P	U	R
T	O	N	T	O		O	T	O		W	A	I	L		C	I	T	E
L	O	T	U	S		R	A	S		O	R	L	Y		R	A	T	E
A	K	I	T	A		E	C	O		N	E	A		T	U	N	E	S
N	A	T	T	Y		M	O	U	N	T	R	U	S	H	M	O	R	E
T	I	L	E			S	T	U		E	V	A						
A	M	E	R	I	C	A	T	H	E	B	E	A	U	T	I	F	U	L
			N	A	T		V	A	L			S	A	N	A			
D	O	N	T	T	R	E	A	D	O	N	M	E		E	R	I	N	S
U	S	U	A	L		L	I	U		D	T	S		L	A	N	E	S
V	C	R	S		H	I	R	E		A	R	T		M	E	T	R	O
E	A	S	T		B	E	E	T		G	E	E		E	L	E	V	E
T	R	E	Y		O	R	S	O		E	E	R		R	I	D	E	S

55

R	E	A	D	S		C	A	Y	S		I	P	O	S
A	T	A	R	I		O	B	O	E		M	I	R	A
N	U	R	S	E	S	A	I	D	A		P	E	E	R
I	D	O		S	E	R	T	A		C	O	C	O	A
S	E	N	A	T	E	S		B	A	R	R			
		N	A	M	E	T	H	A	T	T	U	N	A	
H	A	L	O	S		I	O	N	S		S	I	S	
A	M	E	N		T	A	P	E	S		S	T	N	S
N	I	X		M	O	P	S		U	P	S	E	T	
D	E	L	I	V	E	R	Y	D	A	T	A			
	U	M	P	S		E	M	E	R	G	E	D		
P	A	T	H	S		S	A	L	O	N		O	B	I
E	C	H	O		R	U	B	I	K	S	C	U	B	A
T	H	O	M		O	R	E	S		I	D	L	E	R
E	Y	R	E		B	E	T	H		L	I	D	D	Y

56

```
A S S O C ▪ ▪ ▪ S P A S
R A H R A H S ▪ P O T T E R Y
E Y E D R O P ▪ R E W A R D S
T I E ▪ D O A S I D O ▪ C O T
E T T E S ▪ M O M ▪ A V E R S
▪ S R T A ▪ M A D M E N ▪
O U T R U N ▪ E R E ▪ E T O N
T S O ▪ D I P T Y C H ▪ S T E
B E T A ▪ M A H ▪ C O H O S T
▪ H A W A I I ▪ A U E L ▪
S H E A R ▪ N N E ▪ R E U P S
T O W ▪ O U T G R O W ▪ T R I
E P I S T L E ▪ G R E C I A N
L I N S E E D ▪ S T E P O N E
E N D S ▪ ▪ ▪ K I N K S
```

57

```
L I S T ▪ L O T U S ▪ D C C I
I N C A ▪ U N I F Y ▪ R O U T
E D U C ▪ L E M O N T A R T S
G E R T R U D E S T E I N ▪
E E R I E ▪ ▪ A E N E A S
S P Y C A M ▪ W A X ▪ E L M S
▪ G O B A D ▪ B R I B E
[ROSE] I S A [ROSE] I S A [ROSE] I S A [ROSE]
P R M E N ▪ C A M U S ▪
S E N T ▪ D S T ▪ P O T P I E
I D O T O O ▪ N O O N E
▪ F L O R A L D I S P L A Y
S H O E F E T I S H ▪ H I L O
A M O I ▪ M A R C I ▪ A S I R
K O L N ▪ I D E S T ▪ T H E E
```

58

```
C A M P S ▪ P A G E T ▪ L A P D
A D I O S ▪ A L A M O ▪ O S O S
S H R U G ▪ T O R T R E F O R M
H E A R T T R A N S P L A N T ▪
E R G S ▪ O O F ▪ O A T E R S
W E E ▪ B A L ▪ C T R ▪ M A Y
▪ N O S C O R E ▪ O N A I R
▪ F I R S T A M E N D M E N T ▪
R I C A N ▪ R E D N O S E
E N E ▪ S S N ▪ I N K ▪ M A M
N I S S A N ▪ F S U ▪ S A L E
▪ S T A G E A D A P T A T I O N
S H O E R E P A I R ▪ P A T H S
C E R N ▪ Z O R R O ▪ I S A A C
I S M S ▪ E P E E S ▪ P H I S H
```

59

```
A T P L A Y ▪ U N I ▪ P C T S
D I R I G I B L E S ▪ R A H S
E L E V E N + T W O ▪ O S I S
E S S E S ▪ A R T L O V E R ▪
P I T T ▪ O V A ▪ D R I F T S
▪ T O H A V E ▪ N E E D I E R
▪ M E R L E ▪ E L E A
B I C ▪ A N A G R A M ▪ E N S
E T U I ▪ G A V E L ▪
L A T T I C E ▪ O R I N G S
A D R E N O ▪ Q U O ▪ O R C S
▪ D A M A S C U S ▪ S N O O P
A S T I ▪ T W E L V E + O N E
S U E Z ▪ A T E Y E L E V E L
A P S E ▪ S S N ▪ E L D E S T
```

60

```
H O T ▪ M E O W S ▪ D E V I L
A N A ▪ A L P H A ▪ O V I N E
R E N ▪ D E P O T ▪ L E X U S
M A G L E V ▪ L I K E ▪ E R S
▪ V I S C E R A ▪ K N E E
S I T I N ▪ O T I S ▪ U S S R
T R O I ▪ C A T C H E R ▪
E A R ▪ P A T H ▪ M O D E L A
P E T R O V ▪ E R I N ▪ T A G
▪ B R E E D E R ▪ R O M E
S E M I ▪ A J O B ▪ Z O N E D
A X E S ▪ R E G A L E S ▪
M A N ▪ A T M S ▪ O P E N U P
O C T A L ▪ P O A C H ▪ O L E
A T A L L ▪ L U C K Y ▪ S N L
S A L T Y ▪ O T T E R ▪ E A T
```

61

E	E	E	E			M	A	Y			Q	Q	Q	Q
M	E	D	E	A		A	T	V		C	U	T	I	T
F	O	U	R	L	E	T	T	E	R	W	O	R	D	S
		I	I	I	I		T	T	T	T				
	S	S	E		G	N	A	T	S		I	M	S	
G	E	T	S	T	H	E	R	E		S	N	E	E	R
O	N	E	T	O	T	E	N		J	I	G	G	L	E
O	O	P		A	H	S		F	A	N		A	L	A
D	R	O	I	D	S		G	A	N	G	S	T	E	R
S	A	U	C	Y		A	N	C	E	S	T	O	R	S
	S	T	E		A	R	C	E	D		O	N	S	
		B	B	B	B		O	O	O	O				
R	E	P	E	A	T	O	F	F	E	N	D	E	R	S
I	N	E	R	T		R	E	F		A	B	D	U	L
G	G	G	G			S	Y	S			Y	Y	Y	Y

62

E	L	A	L		R	A	H	S			L	U	L	L
M	I	L	A		I	C	E	T		C	O	P	A	Y
A	B	E	T		P	E	R	O	G	A	T	I	V	E
I	R	R	E	G	A	R	D	L	E	S	S			
L	A	T	T	E		S	E	A	C	A	L	F		
	E	T	N	A		N	R	A		E	R	R		
E	X	C	E	T	E	R	A		F	R	A	U		
P	R	O	N	O	U	N	C	I	A	T	I	O	N	S
E	A	R	S		A	S	T	E	R	I	C	K		
E	Y	E		C	H	O		T	E	A	S			
	S	Y	R	I	A	N	S		M	T	I	D	A	
	C	A	M	E	A	C	R	O	S	S	E	D		
S	U	P	P	O	S	A	B	L	Y		E	S	A	I
K	N	I	T	S		C	R	U	E		E	U	R	O
I	O	N	S		T	E	E	S		D	E	E	S	

63

S	A	L		R	O	I	L		F	E	S	T	S
U	G	O		E	R	N	E		S	I	X	E	R	S
N	I	C	O	T	I	N	E		Y	A	P	P	E	R
S	T	A	N	D	B	Y		O	N	S	E	T	S	
E	A	T	S		I	C	O	N	O	C	L	A	S	T
T	T	O	P	S		R	E	P	O	S	T	E	D	
S	E	R	E	N	A		I	I	S		E	S	S	
		C	O	I	N	F	L	I	P	S				
D	B	L		R	O	I		S	T	O	L	A	F	
W	A	I	T	A	S	E	C		A	R	O	L	L	
I	N	C	O	M	P	L	E	T	E		T	I	T	O
	D	E	N	I	E	S		R	E	M	O	T	E	S
C	A	N	I	N	E		C	O	N	I	F	E	R	S
M	I	S	T	E	D		E	M	I	L		R	E	E
I	D	E	E	S		O	P	E	D		S	D	S	

64

W	E	S	S	O	N		L	I	S		A	L	A	E
A	N	T	E	C	E	D	E	N	T		R	A	S	A
I	D	O	N	T	D	R	I	V	E		E	N	T	S
S	E	C	S			S	I	E	A	G	E			
T	A	K	E	S	5		T	R	A		E	R	O	
S	R	S		A	F	I	R	E		S	O	L	I	D
			E	R	O	S	E		G	A	O	L	S	
	P	A	R	A	L	L	E	L	O	G	R	A	M	
	A	M	I	N	D		L	E	G	I	T			
I	R	E	N	A		A	S	K	O	F		O	V	O
N	O	N		C	A	P			S	T	U	P	O	R
4	D	A	Y		B	I	G	3		N	I	L	E	
T	I	M	E		B	E	O	R	I	G	I	N	A	L
H	E	E	P		I	C	E	S	K	A	T	E	R	S
S	S	N	S		E	E	S		E	L	Y	S	E	E

65

B	E	A	D		S	L	I	P		A	D	I	P
L	P	G	A		T	I	T	L	E		R	E	N	E
A	H	A	B		A	F	O	U	L		I	C	E	D
N	O	P		A	L	T		T	O	E		R	A	E
C	R	E	A	T	E		O	P	E	N	E	R	S	
	P	R	A	T	T		E	R	R	A	N	T		
	A	S	T	A	I	R	E	S		A	S	E	A	
T	N	T		P	R	A	T	T	L	E		E	S	L
I	D	E	D		C	R	U	E	L	E	S	T		
P	R	E	A	M	P		A	N	T	I	S			
S	O	L	D	E	R	S		D	E	S	I	G	N	
O	M	G		T	O	P		A	O	L		R	I	O
V	E	R	O		S	I	N	E	W		H	E	A	D
E	D	E	N		Y	E	A	R	N		E	N	N	E
R	A	Y	E		L	E	O	S		P	E	T	S	

66

P	A	T	M	O	R	E		O	N	E	A	R	T	H
A	R	E	O	L	E	S		B	E	A	N	E	R	Y
C	O	N	N	I	V	E		S	H	U	N	N	E	D
K	O	S	O	V	O		P	E	I		N	E	E	
			C	A	C	T	U	S		I	S	U		
F	E	E	L		T	O	S	S		S	I	G	H	T
L	A	C	E		A	I	M		T	E	R	R	O	R
A	S	I		H	E	L	O	I	S	E		A	W	E
M	E	R	G	E	S		T	O	A		V	E	T	S
E	L	B	O	W		S	T	L	O		E	R	O	S
	Y	O	N		H	O	A	R	D	S				
A	W	N		D	A	B		P	O	S	I	N	G	
B	A	N	G	K	O	K		A	M	N	E	S	I	A
E	V	A	S	I	V	E		D	U	E	L	I	N	G
D	E	F	A	M	E	S		D	R	E	S	S	E	S

67

S	A	B	E		S	O	N	I	C		W	A	L	DO
H	E	L	I		T	R	I	S	H		I	N	O	N
O	R	I	G		O	I	L	P	A	I	N	TI	N	G
W	I	S	H	B	O	N	E		R	L	S			
N	E	S	T	E	G	G		A	L	LA		H	A	S
			N	A	E		A	B	I	T	M	U	C	H
O	L	S	O	N		I	N	SOL	E		A	G	U	A
M	A	T	T	S		N	O	U		F	J	O	R	D
E	Y	R	E		A	FA	S	T		R	O	S	A	S
N	U	I	S	A	N	C	E		H	O	R			
S	P	A		MI	T	T		M	A	S	S	A	G	E
			S	T	S		L	A	S	T	C	A	L	L
J	E	RE	M	Y	I	R	O	N	S		A	R	A	L
U	L	E	E		E	A	S	E	L		L	O	N	I
DO	Y	L	E		R	E	E	S	E		E	N	D	S

68

S	E	W	S		A	M	F	M		A	Q	A	B	A
A	R	O	D		M	I	L	E		S	U	N	U	P
P	R	O	S	C	E	N	I	A		S	A	Y	S	O
H	O	D		O	L	E	G		W	A	Y			
O	R	S	I	N	I		H	A	R	M		B	B	S
		O	S	S	A		T	R	E	S		I	R	E
A	R	R	E	T		B	L	I	N	I		T	A	U
T	H	R	E	E	T	O	E	D	S	L	O	T	H	S
T	E	E		L	I	S	S	E		K	L	E	E	S
A	I	L		L	E	S	S		O	W	A	R		
R	N	S		A	R	A	B		C	O	N	V	E	X
		I	T	S		I	B	A	R		E	V	A	
K	A	U	A	I		P	R	I	S	M	A	T	I	C
I	L	L	G	O		E	D	G	E		M	C	A	T
T	I	E	O	N		I	S	S	Y		O	H	N	O

69

K	A	L	B		U	L	T	I	M	A		J	O	S
I	D	E	A		T	A	I	L	O	R		E	N	O
T	H	E	B	E	A	T	L	E	S	S		T	R	U
S	E	R	A	P	H				S	O	A	P	U	P
C	R	E	W	S		S	O	L	O	N	G	A	S	S
H	E	R	A		K	A	R	O			E	C	H	O
		W	H	A	T	A	G	U	Y		K	E	N	
	T	R	A	I	N	I	N	G	B	R	A	S	S	
D	O	E		M	E	A	T	I	E	S	T			
A	T	M	S		T	E	A	R		R	U	S	T	
W	H	O	C	A	R	E	S	S		R	E	S	A	W
D	E	V	I	S	E				S	O	M	A	L	I
L	E	A		S	H	U	T	T	L	E	B	U	S	S
E	N	L		N	E	S	S	I	E		L	S	A	T
D	D	S		S	M	O	K	E	D		E	A	S	Y

70

S	A	T	C	H	E	L		A	C	T	E	D	U	P
I	N	A	P	I	L	E		B	R	O	M	I	N	E
C	A	T	A	L	O	G		C	O	M	P	A	S	S
			S	O	P	R	A	N	O	S		P	U	T
E	K	G		H	E	L	E	N		H	E	R	E	
T	N	I	O	P	T	S	E	W		P	A	R	E	R
C	O	L	B	E	R	T		S	S	R	S			
S	B	A	R	R	O		✳		O	U	T	A	T	E
			I	S	N	T		T	U	N	E	D	I	N
S	P	R	E	E		E	A	S	T	E	N	D	E	R
L	A	I	N		B	E	R	T	H		S	A	Y	
I	M	F		P	E	T	E	R	P	A	N			
M	E	L	R	O	S	E		A	A	M	I	L	N	E
E	L	E	A	N	O	R		P	R	I	C	I	E	R
S	A	D	N	E	S	S		S	K	E	E	T	E	R

71

```
T A C O   O S A K A   A C A D
O N U P   E P C O T   R O L O
R I P E   D O U B L E P L A Y
A M O N G   O R E   D E I C E
H A L F L I F E   T U L S A N
S L A L O M S   T H C   E R N
      A V E   M O O   M U T E
  T I M E A F T E R T I M E
S I N E   N U N   I A N
O B S   O I L   N U M E R A L
R E P E A T   G A M E F A C E
B R U S H   V E T   D I T T O
A I R Q U A L I T Y   E T O N
T U T U   M A C E D   L E N I
E S S E   O D O R S   D R E D
```

72

```
D A T A   N A M A T H   C P A
E M I T   A R A B I A   H I C
B E T T E M I D L E R   E P H
A L T A R   L E O I   P R E T
S I E R R A   H O N O L U L U
E A R   E X A M   C A B I N
  A P T L Y   P A Y I N G
  I O L A N I   P A L A C E
S O N D R A   D O N A T
A W E E K   P E T E   A S H
M A U N A K E A   L A B R E A
P C P S   H E R A   M A C A W
R I P   B A R A C K O B A M A
A T E   A K I N T O   E R E I
S Y D   G I N N E D   L O D I
```

73

```
E C R U   G L A S S   T E E M
A L U M   S I N A I   E M M A
N O T B Y A L O N G   E M I R
  S A R A   T N T   E L I
L E B A N O N   A S H O T I N
A D A   G U A M   A U T O
G I G A   I M E A N I T
S N A P   J E L L O   D O W N
  H O A R D E R   O C H O
  S H I P   S U V S   C I G
T H E D A R K   T O P H A T S
H U T   H A N   E A S E
U T E P   G U N W E D D I N G
G U R U   A R O A R   J O E L
S P O T   S L I N G   I N D O
```

74

```
A G A S   S C O W S   H A V E
P A C T   N O T R E   O M I T
E S T O   A R R O W S M I T H
S O U P S P O O N   T E T R A
  L A G O O N   G R A T E O N
A I R O F F E N S I V E
U N I   A F R O   B E A G L E
R E E D   S R A   M O O D
A S S I S T   A L T A   I V E
    E E R O S A A R I N E N
C A S T L E D   S L I N G S
E L I S E   D A T E S B A C K
A E R O S O L C A N   O W E N
S U E D   N O T I T   R A N I
E T N A   S T I R S   N Y E T
```

75

```
C R I   C A J O L E D   M E G
L A N   A G E S A G O   A D A
E N T   R O S E S A R E R E D
A D O R E R S   S N A K I N G
R O N I   A E S   G E N I E
C L A S P S   S A S   S E C T
U P T H E   O S T I A
T H E I N V I S I B L E M A N
    H O L S T   A N I M A
T A L L   L Y S   I N A N E R
O P I U M   S G T   T E R R
M O N K E E S   S I B E R I A
C L E A N S H O U S E   A C T
A L A   S T E P I N S   L A E
T O R   A D A P T T O   E N D
```

The New York Times

Crossword Puzzles

The #1 Name in Crosswords

Available at your local bookstore or online at nytimes.com/nytstore

St. Martin's Griffin